YORK NOTES

P a etur

SPIES

 Longman   York Press

The right of Anne Rooney to be identified as Author
of this Work has been asserted by her in accordance
with the Copyright, Designs and Patents Act 1988

YORK PRESS
322 Old Brompton Road, London SW5 9JH

PEARSON EDUCATION LIMITED
Edinburgh Gate, Harlow,
Essex CM20 2JE, United Kingdom
Associated companies, branches and representatives throughout the world

First published 2007

10 9 8 7 6 5 4 3 2 1

ISBN 978–1–4058–6183–0

Phototypeset by utimestwo, Northamptonshire
Printed in China

PART ONE

INTRODUCTION

HOW TO STUDY A NOVEL

Studying a novel on your own requires self-discipline and a carefully thought-out work plan in order to be effective.

- You will need to read the novel more than once. Start by reading it quickly for pleasure, then read it slowly and thoroughly.

- On your second reading make detailed notes on the plot, characters and themes of the novel. Further readings will generate new ideas and help you to memorise the details of the story.

- Some of the characters will develop as the plot unfolds. How do your responses towards them change during the course of the novel?

- Think about how the novel is narrated. From whose point of view are events described?

- A novel may or may not present events chronologically: the time scheme may be a key to its structure and organisation.

- What part do the settings play in the novel?

- Are words, images or incidents repeated so as to give the work a pattern? Do such patterns help you to understand the novel's themes?

- Identify what styles of language are used in the novel.

- What is the effect of the novel's ending? Is the action completed and closed, or left incomplete and open?

- Does the novel present a moral and just world?

- Cite exact sources for all quotations, whether from the text itself or from critical commentaries. Wherever possible find your own examples from the novel to back up your opinions.

- Always express your ideas in your own words.

These York Notes offer an introduction to *Spies* and cannot substitute for close reading of the text and the study of secondary sources.

CHECK THE BOOK

Malcolm Bradbury's book *The Modern English Novel* (1993) is a good introduction to studying modern novels.

CHECK THE BOOK

Frayn's collection of essays, *The Human Touch* (2006), considers many aspects of philosophy, most of them related to science, but some also considering the role and nature of fiction. 'Is it true about Lensky' is about fiction, truth and games.

READING *SPIES*

Spies is a novel which draws on several different literary genres. The main part of the action of *Spies* follows two boys from the 1940s, Stephen Wheatley and Keith Hayward, as they try to unravel a mystery, which at first appears to be of their own making. When they begin to spy on Keith's mother (Mrs Hayward) they are prompted by the fanciful notion that she is a German spy. As the **narrative** progresses, though, we realise that she really does have a hidden secret. As the boys follow and watch her, they uncover clues which are revealed to us at the same rate as they discover them. As in a traditional **mystery** novel, we are not given any privileged information ahead of the boys' discoveries: the boys make deductions, and so do we – though ours are likely to be rather different and our paths of enquiry soon diverge. Even though we are likely to solve the mystery of Mrs Hayward's secret long in advance of Stephen, we will probably still be surprised by the ending and the additional revelations of the **narrator**.

Spies is also a **historical novel**, but with a difference – it is a retrospective account told in the present day. Despite the modern frame, the particular historical period in which the main action takes place is vital to the plot: the story could not be set at any other time. The social attitudes prevalent at the time, combined with the very specific situation of the Second World War, in which a man could be obliged to fly a fighter plane and court-martialled for cowardice if he lost his nerve, make the action of the novel possible.

In addition, *Spies* draws on the tradition of the **coming-of-age novel**. In *Spies*, we see just the beginning of Stephen's adolescence and we have little opportunity to speculate about how the events described have had an impact on his character development and later life. Stephen himself realises that the episode represents something unresolved in his life, but the novel does not go very far towards resolving it. As with the other literary traditions mentioned here, *Spies* is influenced by the coming-of-age genre without belonging to it fully. The novel draws on different strands in literary tradition to elucidate the narrator's thoughts and experiences as he recalls and analyses events from his past.

CONTEXT

Michael Frayn commented in an interview with John Tusa on BBC Radio 3 (4 April 2004) that children do not think about the conditions in which they grow up: 'That's the funny thing about being a child: you take everything for granted, whatever is happening around you that's the way the world is.'

CONTEXT

Stephen and Keith behave at times as though they are starring in their very own *Boys' Own* adventure story. For more on this genre, see **Background: Literary background**.

The narrator of *Spies* is an elderly man reflecting on an episode in his childhood. He is always in the foreground, reminding us of the process of making the story. Ostensibly, he is constructing it from his memories, but our awareness of him throws into relief the process of composition that the novelist is engaged in, too. As the narrator says things and unsays them, changing his mind, we are led to question what is 'real' – what is the 'true' story, if there is one. The novel asks specific questions, through the ponderings of the narrator, about what it is to know something and how well we can rely on memory. There is no definitive answer or conclusion. The narrator is left uncertain as to what he believed, suspecting that he held two or more incompatible beliefs in tension, not challenging the situation or thinking that it needed to be resolved. This means that the entire novel has a feeling of contingency and fragility. We are forced to consider issues such as the reliability of the narrative and whether it has fulfilled its purpose.

There are several layers of composition to *Spies*. The boys Stephen and Keith make up a story about Mrs Hayward which they then try to conjure into reality by finding evidence to support it. The story of this happening is recreated by the narrator from his fractured memories. And the story of his act of construction is created by the author, Michael Frayn, fitting all of this into a carefully built narrative framework. *Spies* was published in February 2002, so Frayn wrote it when he was himself nearly seventy years old – about the same age as the narrator in the novel. There are some autobiographical aspects to the text, including childhood during the Second World War, and the characters of Stephen and Keith. The virtual absence of Stephen's mother from the plot may reflect the absence of Frayn's mother from his adolescence (she died when he was twelve years old).

Spies is a rewarding novel to study, but it can also be challenging. The final chapter contains revelations that force us to re-evaluate what has gone before. On rereading the novel, we are likely to see new significance in some of the incidents, language and imagery. These meanings only become apparent when we know that Stephen's family is German-Jewish. The whole of the novel and our experience of it lurches sideways once we are aware that the

> **CONTEXT**
>
> Michael Frayn has said: 'Stephen is a bit like me as a boy, but his mother's not very much like my mother. But the friend, Keith, is very much like the friend I did have at the time and his parents are very much like the parents that my friend actually had' (interview with John Tusa, BBC Radio 3, 4 April 2004). Stephen seems to be around ten in the early 1940s, so he would have been born about the same time as Frayn.

narrator is not quite who we thought he was and that there was in fact a very different secret at the heart of the novel which we had not anticipated.

As readers, we may feel betrayed as well as unsettled. This sets up a challenging relation to the text, but one which offers fruitful rewards for the careful reader or student.

PART TWO

THE TEXT

NOTE ON THE TEXT

Spies was first published in 2002 by Faber & Faber, London. A paperback edition was published in 2003, also by Faber, and is used in the preparation of these Notes.

Spies has been translated into German and French. It won the Whitbread Novel Prize in 2002.

SYNOPSIS

The main action of the novel is set in one summer during the Second World War. The action is recalled by the elderly **narrator**, who is revisiting the scene of his childhood in an attempt to resolve something that troubles him. He has been reminded of some distant episode by the scent of privet, which he cannot at first identify. He is not sure why he finds the scent so disturbing and decides to investigate by returning to the London suburb where he grew up. The action set in the 1940s is pieced together from his memories as he walks around the road he lived in.

As a child called Stephen, the narrator spent most of his time playing with his friend Keith. Keith and Stephen were both set apart from the other children to some degree: Stephen because he was small and weedy, easily bullied; Keith because he went to a private school and his family was socially superior to the neighbours. Stephen and Keith spend the time in imaginative projects such as trying to build an underground railway system and tracking down an ape-man Keith claims to have seen. A new adventure presents itself when Keith tells Stephen that his mother, Mrs Hayward, is a German spy. The boys begin to follow her and spy on her, looking in her diary and concluding that she goes on secret missions.

The game gets out of hand when it transpires that Mrs Hayward really does have a secret. She visits the nearby railway embankment,

> **CONTEXT**
>
> Privet (*Ligustrum*) is an evergreen or semi-evergreen shrub which bears clusters of small white flowers in late June. There are about fifty varieties of privet. It is often used for hedging in English suburban parks and gardens.

> **CONTEXT**
>
> The date is not specified, but there has been time for the ruins of a bombed house to become overgrown. The bombing of London began in the summer of 1940 and was over by the summer of 1941.

where she hides objects in a concealed box. Uncovering Mrs Hayward's secret is not straightforward, though, as the boys are not very good at following her and decide after a while that she magically disappears and reappears. In fact, she is walking in a direction that it would not occur to them to go in, so they are losing track of her.

The boys share a secret hideout inside a privet hedge and it is from here that they coordinate their spying activities. The hideout is a private kingdom of sorts, in which Keith rules. He bullies Stephen, and both his own confidence in his superiority and Stephen's insecurity work together so that Keith's power over Stephen is unchallenged for much of the novel.

In an attempt to make Keith admire him, Stephen visits the railway embankment alone one night. He finds clothing in the hidden box, but is disturbed by a man who runs away when he discovers Stephen. Keith is not impressed by Stephen's performance, accusing him of cowardice. The two boys go together to the embankment, but the box has been moved. While they are there, though, Mrs Hayward comes through the tunnel. They follow her to a patch of derelict land called the Barns but cannot discover where she goes.

To amuse themselves, the boys throw stones. After hitting a sheet of corrugated iron, they realise that someone is hiding in a space beneath it. They believe it to be an old tramp, and torment him by beating on the metal sheet. They run away when they fear that they may have killed him.

Later that day, Keith's father accuses Keith of taking a thermos flask. The boys realise that Mrs Hayward has taken it to the man she is meeting near the Barns, but they say nothing and Mr Hayward canes Keith. Stephen finds Mrs Hayward to let her know what has happened. Through this episode a bond is formed between Mrs Hayward and Stephen which makes him feel that he has become her accomplice in some way.

A girl from the street, Barbara Berrill, visits Stephen when he is in the hideout. This annoys Stephen greatly at first. He is both afraid of Keith being angry with him and irritated by Barbara's girliness and her intrusion into their private world. Over a number of visits, his attitude towards her softens and the first stirrings of sexual interest, in Barbara and in Mrs Hayward, mark the beginnings of adolescence for Stephen.

Mrs Hayward persuades Stephen to take a letter and a basket of provisions to the man hiding at the Barns. Before Stephen can go, Barbara comes into the hideout. She kisses him, and forces him to uncover the items in the basket. Mr Hayward discovers them and makes Stephen surrender the basket to him. Mrs Hayward's freedom is severely curtailed after this episode.

Stephen, terrified and tormented by guilt, takes provisions from his own house to the Barns. He is forced to talk to the hiding man. He believes the man to be a German airman who has been shot down, but the man knows who Stephen is and speaks perfect English.

Stephen has to agree to carry a token from the man to Mrs Hayward – a silk map of Germany – and give her the simple message 'For ever'. Unable to get access to Mrs Hayward, Stephen decides to conceal the scarf in the hideout. While he is in there, though, Keith comes in. Keith torments Stephen, saying he has broken his oath to keep everything secret, and wounds his throat with a bread knife that they keep in the hideout. In torment, Stephen creeps out of his house at night to try to hide the scarf at the railway embankment. When he gets there, he finds the place busy with men removing the corpse of a man killed on the tracks. He realises that it is the man from the Barns.

In the very last chapter, the narrator sums up, outlining what has happened since in his life and revealing information that casts all that has gone before in a new light. He confirms what readers have probably already suspected, that the man from the Barns was Keith's Uncle Peter, a pilot. Everyone except Mrs Hayward and his wife Auntie Dee (Mrs Hayward's sister) believed him to be flying missions over Europe. Instead he had lost his nerve and deserted, finding refuge near the railway embankment. Whether he and Mrs Hayward were actually having an affair or she simply took pity on

CONTEXT

At the end of the novel we discover that Stephen Wheatley has reverted to his original German name, Stefan Weitzler, since returning to Germany. Weitzen is the German for wheat.

him and his terrible secret remains uncertain. Most surprisingly, the narrator also reveals that his own family is Jewish and had escaped from Nazi Germany before the war, changing their name from Weitzler to Wheatley. His father worked in intelligence for the British.

DETAILED SUMMARIES

CHAPTER 1

- The narrator, Stephen Wheatley, struggles to recognise a scent which prompts a strange, uneasy response in him each year.
- His daughter tells him it is the scent of privet, using its German name 'Liguster'.
- Stephen recalls events of sixty years ago that have caused the scent to have particular resonance for him and decides to revisit London, where he grew up.

In late June, the **narrator** is disturbed by a scent. He is not able to trace it to any of the plants in the gardens that he is walking past, but it makes him feel homesick. He realises that it is familiar from his childhood. He asks his daughter which plant produces the smell and her reply is 'Liguster'; he doesn't recognise the name. He feels that it reminds him 'of something I don't quite like to think about' (p. 4) in his childhood, and it continues to trouble him.

Waking in the night, he realises that his daughter was not speaking English and looks up the word in a dictionary. In Chapter 2 the word is revealed to be privet.

A rush of details from the past comes back to Stephen, prompted by his recognition of the plant. He mentions Keith's mother and Keith, who are both central **characters** in the main action of the novel, and wonders what has become of them, or if they are dead. Then he mentions the six words which 'changed everything' (p. 6). At this point they remain unspoken, creating **dramatic tension** as we naturally want to know what they are. He tells his children that he will go to London for a few days, on a nostalgic trip, but does not tell them the full purpose of his planned visit.

COMMENTARY

The chapter introduces the **first-person narrator**, Stephen Wheatley, who is now an elderly man and will recall the events of his childhood. We learn in this chapter that Stephen has at least two children, a son and a daughter. The son is married; the daughter has two small children but a husband is not mentioned. His daughter visits him weekly, coming by car. He is a professional translator, presumably between German and English, although this is not made explicit here. His profession may conjure up a picture of a quiet and pedantic character, perhaps humble, self-effacing and shunning the public gaze. A translator's role is rarely visible but is that of mediator or facilitator. Here, Stephen will be something like a translator between past and present, though his own presence is more evident to us than that of the translator usually is. It is not revealed at this point that Stephen is living in Germany or that he has changed his name.

The voice in which this chapter is presented is contemplative and slow, giving Stephen's train of consciousness as though he is talking to himself. He asks **rhetorical questions** – 'Which one?', 'And what is it?' (p. 3). He is an old man, perhaps his memory is failing, and the events that trouble him are in the distant past. Sometimes we see him search for words, recreating his struggle to pin down the scent to something in his memory: 'I feel ... what? A restlessness' (p. 3). The chapter moves slowly and there is little activity or **dialogue**. Frequently, an **ellipsis** indicates gaps in Stephen's thoughts or understanding, showing how fragmentary are his memories and thoughts: 'A shower of sparks ... A feeling of shame ... Someone unseen coughing, trying not to be heard' (p. 5). All these are tiny details, which out of context look insignificant. Yet their juxtaposition clearly indicates half-remembered events of some significance, and piques our interest so that we want to know how they are connected and what part they play in the mysterious 'dark and unsettling' (p. 4) thing lurking at the back of Stephen's mind. The cluster of images is followed by the reference to the six words

CHECK THE BOOK

Marcel Proust (1871–1922), *Remembrance of Things Past*, 6 vols, edited by Christopher Prendergast, several translators (2002). *À la recherche du temps perdu* was originally published in seven volumes over fourteen years, 1913–27.

CONTEXT

Stephen can't see or identify the plant that produces the smell. This is the first of many instances of things not clearly seen, identified or understood which becomes an important **motif** in the novel.

CONTEXT

Michael Frayn has himself translated many plays from Russian into English, most of them by Anton Chekhov (1860–1904). Frayn's novel *The Russian Interpreter* (1966) deals with an affair conducted between a British businessman and a Russian woman through an interpreter.

that changed everything. We immediately want to know what the words are, and so are drawn into the story.

The paragraph of a single phrase, 'As words do' (p. 6), alerts us to the importance that words will play in the novel. Stephen's profession of translator is a further indication that the precise meaning of words will be important. It is strange, when we get further into the novel, to find that the young Stephen is particularly inarticulate. And it is this inarticulacy which makes him unable to act to avert the catastrophe that will befall the characters. The opposite of Stephen's statement about words is also true – words can change everything, but so can silence.

The word that is important in this first chapter is 'Liguster', the name of the plant whose scent he is struggling to place. The word itself recalls 'disgust', especially when put with the adjectives applied to the scent by Stephen and his daughter. It 'reeks' (p. 3), it 'insinuat[es] itself so slyly' (p. 4), it is 'vulgar' (p. 4), 'quite harsh and coarse', it 'unsettles' Stephen and 'has a kind of sexual urgency' (p. 3). The English name of the plant, privet, will be important later in the novel, too. The confusion of 'privet' with 'private' and 'privy' becomes a source of humour but also of shame, and prompts some of Stephen's many tongue-tied moments. Even here, he says 'I scarcely like to name it to myself' (p. 6). Although he gives the excuse that 'It's too ridiculous' (p. 6), the real reason may be that it still has awkward and disturbing connotations for him.

Stephen recalls Keith's mother 'laughing at something Keith has written' (p. 5). We will find later that she is laughing at the word 'privet', which Keith has written when he meant 'private'. On a first reading we cannot know this. If we do not know German, or possibly Latin, we will not know either that 'Liguster' is privet. Frayn recreates in us, as readers, the inability to recognise privet that the narrator is experiencing, and makes it suffuse the chapter, as it suffuses the air around Stephen and his memories.

In deciding to revisit London, the scene of the events rekindled in his memory, Stephen is edgy, slightly embarrassed, and he doesn't reveal to his family exactly what he is doing. He extends his son's simple cliché, 'Memory Lane, perhaps' (p. 6), to a full geographic image, where nostalgic recollection is the last sane stopping point 'before you go round the bend and it turns into Amnesia Avenue' (p. 6) – before encroaching madness and then total forgetfulness. In doing this he trivialises what for him will become the serious undertaking of unpicking part of his past and discovering the meanings in events that he could not understand at the time. He mocks his purpose to disguise his unease and uncertainty, but it is to be a necessary exercise in coming to terms with his own past, and the process of growing old. He is aware of 'something ... that remains to be resolved' (p. 6) that he must deal with before the close of his life, and that this may be his last chance.

Stephen has used a dryly humorous image of travel for the flight into the past already, saying 'there are cheap flights to that far-off nearby land' (pp. 3–4) – meaning literally that there are cheap flights to London but metaphorically that there is easy access to his past. The line recalls, quite deliberately, the opening line of the Prologue of L. P. Hartley's novel *The Go-Between* – 'The past is a foreign country: they do things differently there.' (For Stephen, the past is literally as well as metaphorically a 'foreign country'.) *The Go-Between*, like *Spies*, is an account of events in the distant past, told by an old man who as a boy played a part he did not understand in the unfolding of a **tragedy**. There is more about the relationship between *Spies* and *The Go-Between* in **Background: Literary background**.

CHECK THE BOOK

L. P. Hartley (1895–1972), *The Go-Between* (1953).

GLOSSARY

4	Liguster German for 'privet'

CHAPTER 2

- Stephen returns to the town where he grew up, and remembers his past as he walks around the Close where he once lived.
- His recollections create a picture of his childhood and the key characters who will play parts in the coming action of the novel: Keith and his parents, Stephen's own family and Auntie Dee.

- Stephen questions the accuracy of his memories as he prepares to begin his story.

Stephen has returned to his childhood home, and notices that although the layout of the street is superficially the same, numerous details have changed. Many of the distinguishing features of the houses have disappeared and modern additions have made them look similar to one another. In particular, he notices that the scent in the air is of cypress and there is no hint of privet (p. 10).

Many of the triggers to Stephen's memory are not visual, but relate to other senses – like the scent of privet. The noise of the train, which is another memory important later in the novel, is the trigger for the past to 'rematerialis[e] out of the air itself' (p. 10). In his mind's eye, he sees his younger self come out of his house and go to visit Keith, the childhood companion who is to be the other main **protagonist**. Stephen's sense of his own inferiority as a child comes across clearly. His reminiscences reveal the imaginative boyish games and adventures that occupied Stephen and Keith, the relationship between the two and the differences between their two households. They also introduce Keith's parents, Mr and Mrs Hayward; Auntie Dee (Mrs Hayward's sister) and her daughter Milly; and the absent Uncle Peter (Auntie Dee's husband) who is serving in the Air Force during the Second World War; and Stephen's own father and brother. His mother is not included.

Keith's house is impeccable and Stephen finds it intimidating as well as appealing. It is revealed that Keith's parents are at home all the time, Mrs Hayward doing very little, as she has a housekeeper to help her, and Mr Hayward working in his garden and garage. Mrs Hayward is serene, elegant and polite; Mr Hayward is a strict disciplinarian.

Stephen's own house, by contrast, is messy and disorganised. He shares a room with his 'insufferable' (p. 13) older brother who irritates him with his 'supercilious jibe[s]' (p. 13), and the room is filled with a jumble of old bits and pieces and broken toys, nothing like Keith's neat array of boxed toys in working order. Stephen finds his father dull and 'his appearance was as unsatisfactory as Stephen's' (p. 27). To us he appears endearing, though not obviously interesting. There is a clue to there being something more to him in the strange words Stephen reports that he uses, but we are unlikely to be able to make much of these at this point in the novel. Auntie Dee, Mrs Hayward's sister, has a house as chaotic as Stephen's and she is bustling, talkative and kindly. Keith disdains her, assuming the characteristic attitude of half-closed eyelids that becomes a hallmark of his displeasure, yet Stephen sees in her a quintessential 'perfect aunt-likeness' (p. 24).

The **narrator** finally draws back from his reverie and returns to the present and his tour of the Close. He identifies the house that had the bushes whose smell has drawn him back here, and at last reveals that the bushes were privet. He finds their ordinariness embarrassing, given the effect they have had on him. He tries to return to the beginning of his story – the start of the events that will follow – but stalls to examine his memory and how reliable it is. At last, he reveals the words that triggered the main action of the novel: '"My mother", [Keith] said reflectively, almost regretfully, "is a German spy"' (p. 33).

COMMENTARY

The narrator introduces his boyhood self as though he were an entirely separate **character**. He refers to him in the third person, and in the present tense, describing him as he emerges from his house. We see the action unfold as though it were a film, and it takes a few moments to realise that this boy is the narrator earlier in his life. This gives the narrator a chance to present a physical description of himself as a boy, which is important to our later understanding of why he is bullied. It also recreates the sense of the past materialising out of thin air, as the story itself materialises out of nothing, slowly solidifying and gaining colour (p. 15). As he becomes engaged in the story, the narrator switches to the first person, describing Keith as 'my friend' (p. 15). He continues to use both the first and third person to refer to his younger self throughout the novel.

> **CONTEXT**
>
> The Greek philosopher Plato (c. 428–348 BC) believed that everything in the world was an imperfect shadow of an ideal form that could never be achieved. So, for instance, there is an ideal form of 'aunt-ness' which each aunt embodies imperfectly. In Stephen's naive view, everything about Keith is the opposite: a perfect version, an archetype, of the thing it claims to be.

CONTEXT

Some phrases used in the early chapters recur later in the novel where their rephrasing reveals added knowledge or understanding. For instance, Stephen says of Mr Hayward's garage that it had a distinctive scent: 'What was it? Sawdust, certainly, and machine oil. Swept concrete, perhaps. And car' (p. 21). Later, when he has to hand Mr Hayward the picnic basket, he comments: 'The air's full of the smell of sawdust and oil, of concrete and car, and of fear' (Ch. 9, p. 187).

The world of Stephen's childhood is evoked, along with his own feelings about it and himself, through a series of minute observations. This becomes the background to the events that are related in the novel, and many of these tiny episodes are either fleshed out or replayed in the later **narrative**. For now, though, their purpose is to recreate the world of the younger Stephen.

Stephen begins by describing common occurrences rather than specific episodes from his childhood – he used to go over to see Keith, and sometimes he might help clean his bicycle, while at other times they might play in Keith's room. He recreates a wealth of habitual activity with phrases such as 'They might go out for a walk' (p. 18) and 'they might be going upstairs' (p. 17) or 'he may have some chore imposed' (p. 17). Yet the extended recollection of this way of life is given immediacy by the use of the present tense throughout. This gives the impression that we are watching it unfold before us, just as the older Stephen is watching it in his mind's eye. It counterbalances any lack of potency that the use of generalisations may impart. Although Stephen describes things that happened again and again, they are vividly realised.

It comes across clearly that as a child Stephen had the sense that he was inferior to Keith in all respects, and that what Keith did was always right while what Stephen did was always wrong. Everything we are told about Keith's life, house and family is presented as awe-inspiring to the younger Stephen. As readers, we can see the absurdity of a statement such as 'Green's the right colour for a bicycle, just as it's the wrong one for a belt or a bus' (p. 17). Clearly, what makes something right or wrong here is simply whether Keith or Stephen does it. We recognise and **empathise** with the childhood insecurity in Stephen that enables Keith to impose his own 'rightness'. Yet at the same time we see through Stephen's description to interpret the events and words related. Much depends on our greater experience of life as older readers. The features of the style that enable the author to convey both the child's own view and the sinister significance of what he naively relates are discussed in **Critical approaches: Language**.

The characteristic voice of the novel emerges in this chapter as the adult narrator presents events in a voice that could easily be, and that we take to be, that of the child. For instance, when he says 'Barbara Berrill, who's as sly and treacherous as most girls are' (p. 13) we are to understand that this is what a pubescent boy thinks, not what the adult narrator thinks of girls. And when he says of Barbara and her sister 'everyone says they're running wild' (p. 13) this carries the tone of gossip the boy has overheard. 'Running wild' is a phrase that the disapproving mothers in the Close could be expected to use, and that the boy has picked up and included in his vocabulary as he later includes 'the Duration' and 'the War Effort'.

One detail that recurs several times, both in this chapter and later in the novel, is the cloth weighted with glass beads that hangs over the lemonade jug. It becomes a **symbol** or **icon**. The covered jug stands for a whole host of social pretensions clustered around Keith's household. In Stephen's house, the jug of lemonade would be uncovered; in Keith's house, it is given an elegant covering. It is pretty, but rather superfluous, an item of conspicuous and ostentatious ornament that underlines the social difference between the Haywards and their neighbours. In using the cloth, they set themselves apart and show that they aspire or pretend to a grander lifestyle. The English social class system, and the young Stephen's perception of his place in it, provides an important thread in the novel. At the start of this chapter, the **narrator's** account of the houses and their previous inhabitants draws heavily on what the boy thought the social standing was of each household. But the cloth stands also as a symbol of something more sinister. In Keith's house, dark secrets are hidden beneath a shiny veneer of social respectability.

At one point, Stephen corrects himself as he remembers the covered lemonade jug: 'No, wait. I've got that wrong' (p. 31). This raises again the possibility of his memories being inaccurate, and repeats the halting, reflective and questioning style used at the end of the first chapter. The reliability of memory is an important consideration in a novel which is built around events remembered from 'nearly sixty years ago' (Ch. 1, p. 5). He continues to try to piece together his recollections, drawing, like a detective, on details

> **CONTEXT**
>
> Spitfires and Hurricanes (p. 18) were planes used by the Allied Forces in the Second World War, most famously in the Battle of Britain (summer 1940). The reference to Keith's models is, however, **anachronistic**, since the first of the famous Airfix model planes was introduced in 1955. Is this an example of Stephen's memory failing, or of Frayn's research lacking rigour?

> **CONTEXT**
>
> A tablecloth becomes an icon, standing for domestic harmony and unattainable social acceptance, in the adulterous affair depicted in Harold Pinter's play *Betrayal* (1978).

he can remember to try to reconstruct the scene. There is fallen apple blossom, so maybe it is only May; it feels like a weekday. He finally says that what he remembers 'isn't a narrative at all. It's a collection of vivid particulars' (p. 32), and that is exactly what we have been shown on the preceding pages in his evocation of his childhood.

GLOSSARY

9	**prunus** tree of the family that includes plum, cherry and almond. Ornamental prunus varieties, grown for their blossom, are common in middle-class English gardens
10	**homogenised** made identical
10	**coalesced** formed into a solid mass or lumps, from a shapeless or liquid form
10	**cypress** Leyland cypress – a variety of fast-growing conifer commonly used for hedging since the 1970s
11	**pleached limes** lime trees grown so that the branches are intertwined, forming a barrier
11	**render** plaster applied over the brickwork on the outside of a house as a decorative finish
13	**floats** small vehicles or carts; milk floats are now powered by electricity, but during the war they were drawn by horses. Milk and bread were delivered to most houses in England
14	**well pointed** with the mortar between the bricks in good order
15	**ethereal** very delicate and light, with an unearthly quality
16	**Common Entrance** examination taken by children who want to enter a public (privately funded) school
16	**Juice** misunderstanding of 'Jews'
17	**pipeclay** to apply fine, white clay – pipeclay – used to whiten leather
18	**worm gear** toothed wheel worked by a short revolving cylinder with a screw thread
18	**superheterodyne** wireless radio set that produces a signal of its own, which is combined with the incoming signal to produce an intermediate frequency which is then amplified
18	**Paradise** *ironically* named area of wasteland

19	**savannahs** vast areas of tropical or semi-tropical grass plains; used ironically
19	**effrontery** impertinence
20	**dunging** spreading manure on the garden as a fertiliser
20	**rectilinear** containing or moving in straight lines
21	**the Duration** 'For the duration of the war' was a phrase commonly used. It is abbreviated here by Stephen, and elevated by the addition of a capital letter, showing a childish assumption that 'the Duration' was a proper noun and the official term for the war period
22	**meandering** following a twisting path
22	**bayonet** blade attached to the end of a gun, usually a rifle, for assaulting an enemy at close range
23	**game of he** game of 'it' or 'tag'; one player chases after the others and the first one touched then takes over the role of chaser
24	**croquet hoops** metal hoops through which a ball is driven with a wooden mallet in the lawn game of croquet
27	**coodle-moodle** Stephen's childish spelling of the German *Kuddelmuddel*, meaning mess or muddle
27	**shnick-shnack** Stephen's spelling of the German *schnickschnack*, meaning something trivial or unimportant
29	**saccharine** artificial sweetener, often made into very tiny tablets used to sweeten tea or coffee without the calories present in sugar. It is 300 times sweeter than sugar, which is why the tablets are so small
29	**adjutant** helper; it is a military term, meaning a soldier who gives administrative support to an officer
30	**incendiary bomb** a bomb designed to start a fire
30	**Braemar** highland area of Scotland that is a popular holiday resort

QUESTION

Spies is based on the central character's recollection of events, yet at the end of the first two chapters he shows he distrusts his memory. What are the implications of this for the novel?

CONTEXT

The last three letters of WWLTC (p. 28) probably stand for 'lawn tennis club' and the first two denote a local club. Contrary to Stephen's suggestion the letters do not stand for Wimbledon World Lawn Tennis Club, which is in any case not the proper title of the Wimbledon international tennis championships that take place in south-west London every year.

CHAPTER 3

- Stephen and Keith begin to spy on Keith's mother.
- The boys read Mrs Hayward's private diary and discover marks they think indicate secret meetings. She discovers them at her desk and sends them outside.
- Stephen and Keith retire to their hideout in the bushes and Keith makes Stephen swear he will not reveal the details they are uncovering. Keith makes a sign that reads 'Privet' and props it outside the hideout.

CONTEXT

'Careless talk' (p. 39) refers to a series of propaganda posters put up around Britain during the Second World War, each with the slogan 'Careless talk costs lives'. They were intended to stop people talking in public about details which might be useful if overheard by enemy spies. The main effect was to create a culture of paranoia which produced such unfounded suspicions as those of Stephen and Keith regarding Mrs Hayward.

From his adult perspective, Stephen ponders his response, as a child, to Keith's revelation that his mother was a spy. He does not question Keith's authority, and over a few days becomes convinced that Keith is right and that this explains many strange things about Mrs Hayward's behaviour and life in the Close. With some reluctance and anxiety, Stephen joins in Keith's plan of spying on Mrs Hayward and making notes of her daily activity.

Stephen's imagination runs ahead of events, so that he imagines having Mrs Hayward arrested, and how life will change after her arrest. He begins to find suspicious (and more exciting) explanations for many details of the everyday life he sees around him, all of which reinforce his belief that Mrs Hayward is a spy. There is humour in the way that this is presented as the boys find all the mundane details of her day suspicious, while it is clear to us that her activities are wholly innocuous.

While Mrs Hayward takes a nap, the boys creep into the sitting room to look for evidence of her spying activity. Although Keith tries to make something substantial of impressions on the desk blotter, they discover nothing of any note until they find her diary and look through it. Stephen is uneasy at this breach of Mrs Hayward's privacy, as well as anxious about being caught, but is forced by the strength of Keith's character and the hold Keith has over him to take part. The boys find small crosses marked every four weeks, and occasional exclamation marks, which they take as firm evidence of secret activity.

When Mrs Hayward comes into the room and discovers the boys, they are horrified and tongue-tied. She sends them outside and they go to their secret hideout in the privet bushes. There, they talk over what they have discovered and what they should do, Keith taking the lead. Although Stephen comes up with entirely sensible suggestions and objections, he is thoroughly dominated by Keith. Keith forces Stephen to put his hand on the knife which represents to them the bayonet with which Mr Hayward supposedly killed five Germans in the First World War. Stephen repeats an oath devised by Keith, swearing not to reveal their secret on pain of death. Finally, Keith writes 'Privet' on a tile and puts it at the entrance to their hideout.

COMMENTARY

The chapter begins, again, with the adult **narrator** drawing back from the story to question his younger self's response to events. 'How do I react to the news?' (p. 37). His answer to his own rhetorical question is 'I don't think I say anything at all' (p. 37). This both reinforces the conceit of the story as real memories recalled and casts doubt on the accuracy of the **narrative.** He says he 'do[es]n't think' he said anything – but he may be wrong; there is no definitive version of the truth that can now be recovered. He continues to narrate the events immediately after the revelation in this distanced manner, though he is speaking in the first person. The reiterated uncertainty gives the impression of current action observed through fog, or a steamed-up window: it is happening before us, but indistinctly perceived.

Over the ensuing days, Stephen begins to accept Keith's assertion that Mrs Hayward is a spy. In a child-like way, he begins to explain perfectly ordinary happenings by reference to this new 'knowledge'. This process is presented with gentle **irony**. As readers, we know that someone may have a torch on their table for many reasons besides signalling to enemy pilots. Stephen's mistaken imaginings are not ridiculed. They come across as typically childish in their eagerness to make an exciting story from nothing – 'It even beg[an]

CHECK THE NET
www.homesweet homefront.co.uk explains the 'careless talk' campaign and shows the posters. On the home page, click on the 'Careless Talk' link.

CONTEXT
Keith's and Stephen's parents would probably have been in their thirties during the Second World War. This makes them old enough to have lived through the First World War, too. If Mr Hayward fought in the First World War, he would have been born around 1900 and be in his early forties at the time the action is set.

to make sense of a number of things … that I hadn't realised didn't make sense before' (p. 39). Yet we know that these are not plausible explanations.

By presenting the boys' previous adventures in the same deadpan style as their beliefs about Mrs Hayward, the **narrator** undermines the credibility of their 'discovery'. The earlier projects – such as building a transcontinental railway or uncovering a neighbour as a serial killer – are clearly absurd flights of boyish imagination brought about by their desire for excitement. Initially, the narrator makes no distinction between these and the latest adventure. The effect is to show us that to the boys they are equivalent – the identification of Keith's mother as a German spy is no more or less fanciful than the plan to construct a railway line. Later, writing in a voice more closely aligned with Stephen as a child than Stephen as an adult, the narrator tries to distance this new adventure from their earlier fantasies. 'Never before, though, has it ever become real, not really real, in the way that it has this time' (p. 53). He knows, deep down, that they can't make a railway, but this time it could be true.

The chapter reveals more about Stephen's **character** and new, often unsettling, details about Keith. Stephen's low self-esteem is **pathetic**. There is a genuinely sad tinge to the writing as the narrator depicts his former self as quite lacking in either confidence or any sense that he might be a valuable or interesting person. Particularly touching is his suspicion that Mrs Hayward's 'incomprehensible niceness' (p. 39) towards him was just a cover for her secret life. He is easily cowed by Keith, and is unable to stand up to him. Stephen ends up colluding in the invasion of Mrs Hayward's privacy because he is afraid of Keith ridiculing him. Yet his unease is evident. He feels the reproach of the photographs of the adults, yet cannot bring himself to defy Keith. He does not point out Keith's misspelling of 'Private', convincing himself that it doesn't really matter – 'the sense of it is plain enough' (p. 57). Fine aspects of Stephen's character – his moral integrity, his learning, his feeling for others – are denied expression because of Keith's domineering nature and Stephen's fear of him.

The hideout is a special place, a separate world with its own rules. It is a space where the boy's imaginations can run free, where they are outside the authority of adults. Stephen wonders what would have happened if instead of going to the hideout they had been allowed to play indoors. The implication is that the plan would not have taken off as extravagantly if they had been in a domestic setting rather than the wild, free setting of the hideout. Going into the hideout they cross 'the frontier into another country altogether' (p. 52). As well as the hideout, this chapter introduces the bread knife which stands in for Mr Hayward's bayonet. In the strange world of the hideout, the bread knife is the equivalent of the bayonet, but more than this it 'is' the bayonet in the same way, it is suggested, that the bread and wine of Holy Communion 'are' the body and blood of Christ (p. 55). (There is more about religious **imagery** in **Critical approaches: Language**.)

CONTEXT

Holy Communion is the consumption of the communion wafer and wine representing the body and blood of Christ. It is part of the Christian rite of the Eucharist.

In the hideout, Keith makes Stephen feel uncomfortable and stupid by encouraging him to think aloud, interpreting what they have discovered and deciding what they should do, all the time hiding his own superior knowledge. The intention – which succeeds – is to make Stephen think at first that he is ahead of the game and is leading Keith, then to be crushed by realising that Keith is, as usual, ahead of him. Keith's reasoning powers and insight are endorsed by this tactic, and his power over Stephen is reinforced. After establishing his supremacy again, Keith seals his position by making Stephen swear an oath of secrecy. Keith's behaviour borders on bullying, and Stephen notices reminders of Mr Hayward in the way Keith looks at him and how he behaves. As we later learn, Mr Hayward is a sadistic bully who canes Keith and dominates his wife. Aspects of his character are alarmingly present in Keith, who similarly intimidates and dominates Stephen, and threatens him with violence with the bread knife if he reveals their secrets.

In Mrs Hayward's diary, the boys discover 'x' marks every four weeks. The boys do not recognise the 'x' marks as indicators of Mrs Hayward's menstrual cycle, though we as readers do. They similarly misinterpret the exclamation marks. Although their meaning is never made explicit, the implication is that they indicate sexual

CONTEXT

In the days before reliable contraception, it was common to record sexual activity to help with dating any pregnancy that resulted.

activity with Mr Hayward (one instance is on her wedding anniversary). There is a gulf between the adult and child worlds, poignantly highlighted here. It is also a gulf between childhood in the 1940s and childhood today. Modern boys, with the benefit of sex education in schools, would be more likely to recognise the pattern of twenty-eight days.

GLOSSARY

37	**gloaming** poetic term for twilight
45	**Sioux** indigenous North American tribe
46	**tuppenny-halfpenny stamps (pronounced 'tuppny ha'pny')** stamps costing two and a half old pence each (equivalent to 1p in the decimal currency used in the UK since 1971)
51	**tintinnabulations** sounds produced by pealing of bells
55	**Empire Day** 24 May, the anniversary of the birth of Queen Victoria; now renamed Commonwealth Day. The British monarch had the title Emperor (or Empress) of India until 1947
55	**the King's birthday** the birthday of King George VI, 14 December

CHAPTER 4

- During the school week, Stephen and Keith are unable to spy on Mrs Hayward successfully.
- On Saturday, the boys follow Mrs Hayward to Auntie Dee's house and then again when she comes out, but she apparently vanishes.
- Stephen follows Mrs Hayward on his own, and again she disappears at the corner of the road.
- For days, they watch Mrs Hayward but see nothing suspicious, and then one evening she apparently vanishes again.

At school, Stephen is unable to concentrate and drifts into daydreams about Mrs Hayward and her spying activities. He gets into trouble from teachers, and is routinely teased and bullied by boys at school. The school week affords little opportunity for spying on Mrs Hayward. On Friday, Stephen is not allowed out but has to talk to his father, which he resents and finds dull.

On Saturday, the two boys spend the day in the bushes noting down the comings and goings in the Close and making up suspicious excuses and circumstances for the everyday activity they witness. Stephen becomes bored and impatient and stops believing that Keith's mother is a spy.

Mrs Hayward appears and the boys give up bickering, taking renewed interest in her. They follow her, wait outside Auntie Dee's house, then see her walk up the road. When they get to the corner, she has disappeared. Later, she re-emerges from Auntie Dee's house. The boys are confused and disconcerted. They make up fanciful explanations – perhaps she has a time machine or a rocket. They dismiss the possibility that she could have gone into one of the houses on the Avenue inhabited by their social superiors. They investigate their ideas that she could have crawled into a manhole or through a hole in the fence, but are left puzzled.

Again, the older **narrator** expresses doubts about the order of events. He recalls the policeman, then wonders if there were actually two policemen. He remembers Uncle Peter, surrounded by children and falling blossom. The next few times they follow Mrs Hayward, her trips are unremarkable. Many days pass when nothing suspicious happens and they begin to doubt their earlier observations.

Barbara Berrill, one of the girls in the Close, discovers the two boys in their hideout. They refuse to tell her what they are doing, and in revenge she tries to shame them by publicly announcing that they are spying. They feel unable to leave until they are certain she has left the street, and so are still there late enough to see Mrs Hayward make an evening trip along the Close. Again, she disappears at the corner and later re-emerges from her own house to tell Keith off for staying out too late. She is nervously slapping at something on her clothes and later wipes her hands as though they are sticky. Stephen

CONTEXT

Stephen scrapes his unwanted food into a pail to be fed to pigs and later refers to the pig buckets Mrs Hayward passes (p. 71). The pig pails were encouraged by a Ministry of Food advertisement that tried to show how small actions made a valuable contribution:

'Because of the pail, the scraps were saved,

Because of the scraps, the pigs were saved,

Because of the pigs, the rations were saved,

Because of the rations, the ships were saved,

Because of the ships, the island was saved,

Because of the island, the Empire was saved,

And all because of the housewife's pail.'

realises that her hands are not sticky, but slimy, and guesses where she has been. Mrs Hayward takes Keith home, where he will be punished by his father for staying out.

COMMENTARY

It never occurs to Stephen and Keith that Mrs Hayward might turn not towards the shops but in the opposite direction when she reaches the corner. Stephen says: 'There's only one way to go when you get to the end of the Close and that's left, because if you go right the roadway peters out almost at once into a rough track' (p. 71). It escapes his notice (as a child) that even in saying this he is telling us that it *is* possible to go right along the rough track. It is inconceivable to him and Keith that Mrs Hayward would take this path – just as it is inconceivable that she would go into one of the houses on the Avenue. It seems more likely to them that she would crawl into a manhole or through a hole in a fence or even have a rocket or a time machine. This reflects their own behaviour – they would be more likely to crawl into a manhole than go into an area in which they felt socially out of place (whether the elevated Avenue or the inferior Lanes). They project their own feelings onto Keith's mother, who in fact would probably find the Avenue less daunting than a manhole.

Stephen's father and brother are described during the course of the action for the first time in this chapter, though both have been mentioned by the narrator in a retrospective passage in Chapter 2. Stephen finds it annoying that he has to stay in on Fridays to be with his father, and finds his father difficult to talk to. He does not know what to say and becomes tongue-tied. His father seems kindly and genuinely interested in his son's life, though there is a gulf between them. Stephen does not share information with his father and does not know how to respond to his interest. Mr Wheatley quizzes his son, not realising that he is making him feel uncomfortable despite his kindly intentions. Stephen's brother, Geoff, speaks plainly and is a voice of reason. He says outright what we have gathered, accusing Stephen of engaging in 'Another little game your barmy pal's dreamed up' (p. 62).

Uncle Peter, seen in photographs before this chapter, is brought to life in Stephen's recollection of his visit home on leave. Stephen paints an idyllic picture of a war hero among a cluster of adoring children, a picture marked out by its stunning colours and the sound of laughter. It seems altogether unreal. It conjures up an heroic image that Stephen could have borrowed from a war propaganda poster. It bears no relation to the reality of war, and the demoralised, frightened or emotionally destitute men who returned from tours of duty or deserted – a reality which, in fact, lies at the heart of the novel. The war is distant for the boys, however. There are only a few signs of its existence in the Close, making it all the easier for them to construct a fanciful world in which Mrs Hayward is a German spy.

QUESTION

Compare the idealised description of Uncle Peter in this chapter with the broken man he appears in Chapter 10.

CONTEXT

Stephen's reference to the pig bins as the 'War Effort' (p. 71) is a misappropriation of a phrase which covered many types of behaviour British people were asked to adopt to help the country's 'war effort'. The war effort was the coordinated social and industrial response to the war. It involved such varied aspects as women working the land, factories being used to produce ammunition, families being encouraged to 'make do and mend' rather than buying new items, and the rationing of food and clothing.

GLOSSARY

61	**Morse key** a tapper used to send Morse code – a signalling code made up of long and short intervals between taps representing dots and dashes
71	**War Effort** measures the British public was called on to adopt to help the nation in its war against Nazi Germany
72	**circulating library** a library which takes books to people in different localities
79	**scot and lot** a form of tax originating in the Middle Ages and collected from members of a community according to their ability to pay

CHAPTER 5

- The narrator returns to the present again, exploring the changed landscape and contemplating how the area developed.
- Back in the past, Stephen and Keith realise that Mrs Hayward goes through the tunnel in the embankment. They find a large tin box with a packet of cigarettes hidden inside.

- In the hedge, Stephen waits for Keith but is visited instead by Barbara Berrill who tells him that Auntie Dee has a boyfriend and has been seen kissing him by the tunnel.
- Mrs Hayward finds Stephen in the hideout. She asks him not to spy on people and not to lead Keith astray.

The present-day **narrator** is walking around the area of his old home again, and explains how the settlement grew up, carved out of the old farmland to provide new housing in the 1930s. He recalls that beyond the old railway line the land was quite wild and derelict, but discovers that there is now a complex of residential roads and that the tunnel through the embankment itself is now broad, well lit and paved. As the narrator remembers the previous state of the tunnel, he recalls 'brushing at the foul exhalations' left on his shoulder and 'wip[ing] the dark-green slime' from his hands (p. 89), making us realise that this is what Mrs Hayward was doing last time she was mentioned.

In the past once more, Stephen and Keith have realised that Mrs Hayward goes through the tunnel. Despite their fear of the area which lies beyond the boundary of their territory, they go to investigate. Once they have climbed up the embankment, they are frightened by the approach of a train yet they are unable to retreat because at the same time they are aware of Mrs Hayward coming through the tunnel (p. 92). Stephen is keen to escape as soon as she and the train have gone, but Keith is determined to investigate. In the undergrowth, they find a long metal box that once held a croquet set – the croquet set now rusting on Auntie Dee's lawn (Ch. 2, p. 24). Stephen makes the connection between the two while talking to Barbara Berrill (p. 99), and realises that Auntie Dee is involved in the mystery somehow. Inside the box is a packet of cigarettes with a slip of paper bearing an 'x'.

The 'x's on the paper, in the diary, at the ends of his mother's letters and in his algebra problems swim around in Stephen's head and give him bad dreams. 'X', the unknown quantity in an algebraic equation, comes to stand for the unknowns in the mystery the boys are investigating.

Stephen waits in the bushes for Keith, who does not come. Instead, Barbara Berrill comes into the hideout. This shocks Stephen, who does not know how to respond. He claims to dislike her and her girlish ways, but is strangely intimidated by her and fascinated by her strange girlishness. She humiliates him by suggesting he does not know what 'privet' means and by pointing out his embarrassed responses. She tells him that Auntie Dee has a boyfriend, and that her own mother does, too. She is more worldly-wise than he, she knows something about adult sexuality and is amused by his ignorance. Stephen is increasingly tongue-tied and longs for the encounter to end. Worse, Mrs Hayward comes out of the house and he cannot follow her as he can't escape from Barbara.

The next time Stephen is waiting for Keith, Mrs Hayward crawls into the hideout. This embarrasses and confuses Stephen even more: 'I'm too embarrassed to watch her as she struggles in … I know she has to make an awkward spectacle of herself' (p. 105). He does not know where to look and is unable to respond to her questions, being struck dumb by fear and embarrassment. Mrs Hayward tells Stephen, as politely as possible, that it is rude to spy on people and that he and Keith must not follow people around. She astonishes him by saying that Keith is easily led, showing an almost incredible degree of ignorance about her own son's character. She finally makes him promise that he won't disappoint her by disobeying or by telling Keith that she has spoken to him. Stephen mutely agrees. When Mrs Hayward walks down the street towards the tunnel a few minutes later, Stephen knows that he can't follow her.

COMMENTARY

This chapter contributes a lot to our understanding of Stephen and the degree to which he is restricted by his social position and his low opinion of himself. He is compelled to follow Keith's lead, and to return to the embankment to investigate the metal box when he desperately wants to leave. In the hideout, he is unable to tell Barbara Berrill to go away as he is too astonished at her intrusion to be able to act at all. He is deeply ashamed and embarrassed when he confuses the word 'privet' with 'privy' and imagines that this is what first Barbara and later Mrs Hayward understand by Keith's misspelt sign. He is unable to look at Mrs Hayward because he

---

CONTEXT

Electric-diesel trains took over from steam trains in most of Britain during the 1950s. Much of the London metropolitan railway was electrified in the 1930s. The electric trains in the novel would have run on two normal rails and used a third, live, rail to supply the electric current. Most modern trains do not require a live rail as the electricity is generated on board.

CONTEXT

A privy was an outdoor toilet. In the 1930s, many British houses still had outdoor toilets, sometimes shared between several houses, particularly in slum areas. Stephen lives in a street of newly built houses, which would have had indoor toilets.

imagines her embarrassment at being in an ungainly position, crouching on the floor, covered in bits of stick and leaf. He is afraid he will look at her bosom, and too frightened to speak to her. Mrs Hayward exploits his sense of social propriety and responsibility, saying 'I know you're a sensible, well-brought-up boy' and 'So, you see, I'm trusting you. I'm putting you on your honour. Yes?' (p. 109). It has the desired effect because even though he says nothing in response he later feels 'I as good as gave her my word' (Ch. 6, p. 114).

CHECK THE BOOK

Faye Gardner's *Home Life in the 1930s and 40s (Family Scrapbook)* (2005) shows what childhood and home life were like at the time Stephen and Keith were growing up.

Stephen clings to social propriety as his lifeline, and his only guide in the incomprehensible social world. His complete confidence in the social order has been revealed already. He is certain that the social position of his family is low, and that it would be ridiculous to suppose that Keith might ever come to his house. In the same way, it is inconceivable to him that Mrs Hayward might go into one of the houses in the Avenue. When social propriety is breached, he is outraged and confused. He cannot understand why Mrs Hayward is speaking to him about something that he has done with Keith, for 'Everyone knows you tell your own child off, not somebody else's, for offences they've committed together' (p. 107).

Stephen feels constantly tested by 'the long examination board of childhood [that] will last for ever' (p. 96). Every aspect of life is a trial. He doesn't complain about this, any more than he complains about the bullying he endures at school. He simply accepts that this is the way life is. It is the unquestioning acceptance of the scapegoat, the weaker party, and of the child of the 1940s for whom there was commonly little adult concern. Even Stephen, though, is astonished that Mrs Hayward could suspect him of leading Keith astray. It is inconceivable to him that she should know so little about her own son. The juxtaposition of her quick portrait of Keith with Barbara's condemnation of him throws the **character** of the absent Keith into relief. Mrs Hayward says Keith finds it hard to make friends; Barbara says he is universally disliked. Stephen, who beneath his rather frenzied and clingy friendship is aware of Keith's failings, realises that there is truth in Barbara's assessment of Keith as 'stuck-up' and 'horrible' (p. 99):

I can feel the words 'horrible' and 'hates him' taking hold somewhere inside me like germs, in spite of myself, and I know the infection from them will gradually creep through me like the sour dullness of a slow fever. (p. 99)

Despite the sympathy we feel for Stephen, there is a lot of humour in this chapter. The older **narrator** is gently mocking of his former self. He does not demand that we side with him against his aggressors or are sentimental in our view of him. We, too, laugh at his misunderstanding of privet/privy and there is sufficient distance between us and Stephen to find his discomfiture in the hideout amusing as he struggles to avoid looking at any bosoms or revealing the level of his ignorance about adult behaviour – 'What's she talking about? How can someone's aunt have a boyfriend?' (p. 101).

Amongst the comedy, important information is revealed in this chapter. Mrs Hayward is visiting the railway embankment and apparently leaving things for someone. This is the first solid evidence that something is going on. The secret activity is not, after all, something entirely concocted by Keith and Stephen. It becomes clear that Auntie Dee is somehow involved in whatever Keith's mother is doing. That she was kissing someone, and that person has been seen by the neighbours, broadens the mystery into the wider community. Yet that Barbara Berrill knows about it makes Stephen and Keith look faintly ridiculous – even Stephen's brother knows about it.

> **CONTEXT**
>
> 'Gamages of Holborn' (p. 93) refers to the shop A W Gamage Ltd, at 116–28 Holborn, in London. It opened as a small watch repair shop in 1878 and had grown into a large department store by the 1940s. It was renowned for selling a wide range of goods, all very cheaply. The shop closed in 1972.

GLOSSARY

86	**adopted** taken into public ownership; private roads built by developers on new housing estates are maintained by local councils only after they have been adopted
86	**dryshod** with dry feet
87	**postern** a small gate or door for private use
88	**catty stink** the flowers of the elder tree have a distinctive smell like cat urine
88	**billy** billycan; metal pot for boiling water or cooking food over a campfire
92	**gangers** foremen who lead gangs of labourers

continued

92	**ballast** crushed rock used in the foundations of a railway track
92	**chairs** iron or steel cradles attached to a railway sleeper and which holds the rail
92	**bogies** groups of four or six wheels that support each end of a railway carriage
94	**untenanted reliquary** a jewelled case intended to hold the relics of a saint, but empty

CHAPTER 6

- Stephen wakes in the night and goes to the railway embankment in the light of the full moon.
- He is seen by someone, while discovering clothes in the hidden box. Terrified, he dares not glance at the person, but escapes with a sock he has taken from the box.
- Keith is not impressed by Stephen's adventure. When they return to the railway embankment the metal box has gone. They follow Mrs Hayward into the wasteland beyond the railway embankment, but lose her.
- The boys amuse themselves throwing stones, and realise someone is hiding in a disused cellar under a sheet of corrugated iron. They beat the iron roof with a plank and an iron bar, then – afraid they have killed the tramp they believe is hiding beneath it – they run off home.

CONTEXT

Householders were obliged to cover their windows with blackout cloth that blocked all light from inside because lights showing up in the night could guide German bombers to towns.

Stephen wakes in the night and finds the outside world bathed in unearthly moonlight. Despite his terror, he decides he must go to the railway embankment. Once he is there, though, the moon goes behind a cloud and he is stranded in darkness. He finds the metal box and discovers that it contains clothes. He is terrified to realise that someone is approaching him.

Suddenly, the cloud clears and the person who was behind sees Stephen, gasps and runs off. Stephen is too afraid to turn round and look, and later berates himself for this display of cowardice, as he considers it. Terrified, he runs back to the Close where his parents are out looking for him. At home he is in trouble, but finds that he is holding a darned sock that he has taken from the metal box.

The next day he relates his adventure to Keith, who is not impressed. Stephen realises that Keith will not allow him to shine: 'He's the one who's the hero of our projects, not me' (p. 121). The two boys go together to look in the metal box and find that it has gone. Keith berates Stephen for his cowardice, cruelly teasing and goading him, but, when they realise Mrs Hayward is approaching, they both lie face down in the grass, terrified of being discovered. They follow her towards the wasteland and the Lanes, an area of run-down houses inhabited by poor people.

The boys are afraid of the dogs and children they have to pass, but don't see Mrs Hayward. They fall to throwing stones in an overgrown area known as the Barns. When one of the stones hits a piece of corrugated iron, they discover that the sheeting covers an old cellar and someone is hiding in it. They assume it is an old tramp who had been removed from the area the previous year and proceed to torment him by beating on the roof with a plank and an iron bar. When they fear they have killed the tramp, they run back to the Close. Mrs Hayward arrives soon after them. She realises it was Stephen and Keith who were beating on the iron sheet and expresses her disappointment with Stephen.

COMMENTARY

Stephen's poor opinion of himself and his subservience to Keith are further developed in this chapter. He is understandably afraid to go out in the night, and to look at the man who has come up behind him at the railway embankment, yet he is unforgiving in his condemnation of his own behaviour. He correctly anticipates Keith's disgust, and Keith does indeed taunt him and call him a baby when it becomes clear to him that Stephen was too afraid to look at the man. But Stephen has internalised Keith's view of him, and castigates himself before Keith has a chance to. Consequently, he does not see anything unfair in Keith's treatment of him – a common characteristic in people who are repeatedly bullied. The

---

CONTEXT

The development of the area beyond the Lanes had been begun before the war. No residential construction work was carried out during the war, however, as all materials and labour were required by the armed forces. The plan of 'avenues and cul-de-sacs, of roundabouts and turning circles' (p. 128) has been realised by the time the older Stephen revisits the area.

CONTEXT

The Home Guard (p. 132) was a defence force drawn from male volunteers not drafted into the army. Formed on 14 May 1940, it grew within days to number many thousands of men. It was sometimes criticised for being disorganised and amateurish, the men armed with whatever weapons fell to hand.

CONTEXT

The sock in the metal box is dark blue, we discover later when Stephen is able to look at it (p. 120). Although we are not aware yet that the owner of the sock is Uncle Peter, Frayn shows us here that the 'stranger' has been in hiding long enough to be using civilian clothing – the socks issued to members of the Royal Air Force (RAF) were blue-grey.

ease with which he perceives the criticism of others makes Mrs Hayward's quiet rebuke 'Oh, Stephen!' (p. 133) immensely effective in arousing feelings of guilt in him.

Yet Stephen is quite brave. He has an inner compulsion to prove to himself as well as to Keith that he can do things: 'Now I've thought the thought, I know I have to do it. ... I'm going to do it' (p. 115). Stephen hopes he can make amends: 'one single heroic deed ... all my weaknesses and errors wiped away' (p. 114). Although frequently paralysed by fear, he still goes ahead – outside into the night, along the Close, through the tunnel, touching the germ-filled slime (p. 115), putting his hand into the box (p. 116). His one failure is not to look up at the man, and this he sees as confirming his innate cowardice. He judges himself too harshly, just as he knows Keith will.

Stephen is not yet so dominated by Keith that he is blind to the unfairness of Keith's refusal to acknowledge what he has achieved. Even so, Stephen depicts himself as so menial that he is like a dog or a supplicant, dropping tributes and offerings before Keith who will never be satisfied with them. He is both aware that Keith is being unjust and that he is abjectly abasing himself – yet he can't help his behaviour because he is desperate for Keith's approval. It is inevitable that Keith will not be pleased with Stephen's action, as Keith always has to be the one who appears clever, brave, the leader, and the only one who achieves something. Stephen is aware of this, even as he still struggles hopelessly to gain Keith's approval. But there is some comfort for Stephen, too, in seeing even Keith scared, both at the approach of his mother through the tunnel and later when they are afraid they have killed the 'tramp'.

The incident with the supposed tramp is revealing. Stephen is immediately transformed into a bully himself, and there is no hint of shame in his enjoyment of tormenting the hidden man: 'I can't help laughing at the thought. I can't wait to see the comical terror on the old man's face' (p. 131). He relates this as though the event and his feelings are quite ordinary and unremarkable. There is no hint of tension, regret or horror. The callousness of the action shines through the ordinary, dispassionate narration and is made more awful by the calm, measured tone.

Stephen's behaviour is quite horrifying, yet it is convincing. People who are bullied often take the first available chance to inflict abusive behaviour on those who are even less powerful. This is why Keith abuses Stephen, and why Stephen in his turn is elated by realising that the 'tramp' is 'scared of me. He's that low in the table of human precedence' (p. 130). The horrible dynamic of abuse is instantly played out before our eyes, as Stephen takes revenge for his own treatment on the hidden man. Only after they are exhausted does the enormity of what they are doing dawn on the boys. Stephen tries to deny the possible consequences of his actions: 'The old man's not dead, though. How could he be dead? People don't die from a bit of teasing!' (p. 132). The boys respond in the only way they know how – they run away. Neither is able to take responsibility for their actions and confront what they might have done.

CONTEXT

Looking the other way, turning away from the truth, is a recurrent theme in the novel. It is the whole nation's refusal to acknowledge the fear and suffering of men in the armed forces that means Uncle Peter has to hide when he is unable to face flying any more (see Chapters 10 and 11).

GLOSSARY

126	mangles presses for squeezing the water from clothes and linen that have just been washed
128	cul-de-sacs residential roads that come to a dead end, usually with a turning circle, rather than connecting with other roads

CHAPTER 7

- The narrator looks at the space where the bushes once grew and wonders what the child Stephen thought as he hid there.
- Back in the past, Stephen waits for Keith to come to the bushes, but he never does. Eventually, he goes to Keith's house.
- Keith does not engage with Stephen at all but goes about his tasks as though Stephen is not there.

- Mr Hayward comes out of the garage and demands the thermos flask, which he believes Keith has taken. When Keith doesn't respond, Mr Hayward canes his hands.
- Stephen heads for the railway embankment where he bumps into Mrs Hayward and manages to communicate to her what has happened.

The **narrator** is standing outside the house built on the patch of wasteland that was once the site of the bombed ruins of Miss Durrant's house. A tub of geraniums stands where he estimates the hideout in the bushes was. A boy watches him from the window and the narrator is aware that the boy is doubtless suspicious of him. The older man decides that his younger self did not see conflicts between the different beliefs he held and did not examine those beliefs.

Returning to the 1940s, Stephen eventually gives up waiting for Keith to come to him and he goes to Keith's house. Mrs Hayward lets him in, with no suggestion of reproach. Stephen goes up to Keith's room, but Keith will not play with him. He tidies his toys and goes to clean his cricket kit, whereupon Stephen says he will go home. Before he has time to leave, Mr Hayward comes out of his garage and says, cryptically, 'Thermos' (p. 145). It emerges that the thermos flask is missing and he believes that Keith has taken it. Both Stephen and Keith realise that Mrs Hayward has taken it but they say nothing. Finally, Keith is caned for both taking it and not admitting to take it. There is an embarrassing scene, when Stephen sees Keith after the caning, and then Stephen runs to the railway tunnel hoping to find Mrs Hayward. He runs into her and the two of them struggle not to fall into the water in the tunnel. She tells him off, but eventually he gets through to her – though he is again tongue-tied – that the missing thermos flask has caused a problem. She guesses the rest of the situation and hurries home.

COMMENTARY

The narrator wonders how the mind that was once the boy's has now become the man's and yet is inaccessible to him: 'The thing that's so difficult to grasp is that it's the very same head as the one that's here on my shoulders thinking about it' (p. 138). There's a parallel, which he doesn't make explicit, between the geraniums which have filled the physical space occupied by the hideout and the hidden children, and the current mind occupying the physical and mental space of his mind as a child. Things in the past – bushes and thoughts – are somehow still shadowy presences. They are real enough to have drawn him back here and to enable him to recreate the story he is telling.

Woven into this unexamined concern with time is an **epistemological** question about the nature of knowledge and understanding. The narrator does not give a rigorous philosophical discussion of the issue. Rather, he raises the question, and lets it hang unanswered: 'I'm not sure … if I really understand even what it means to understand something' (p. 138). Reflecting on the geraniums, he feels he doesn't need to understand because 'I've got the general story' (p. 138). This seems to be his attitude to the entire narrative. He is abdicating any responsibility for understanding and explaining events – instead he will proceed to tell them and let any meaning (if events have any meaning) emerge from the story.

The narrator's consideration of understanding gives no insights to help us with the story, and looks initially like a dead end. Yet it sets out a manifesto for the author. Can human action ever be fully understood, even our own actions? The novel is largely about misunderstandings – the stream of attempts at interpretation that Stephen and Keith make, all misguided, leads to tragedy. No events are clearly seen, none is truly understood. The whole novel is about the narrator's struggle to understand what has happened and how it has shaped his life.

The narrator suggests that Stephen did not really think about what Mrs Hayward was doing, and saw no conflict between the different ideas he held even when they clearly contradicted each other. Just as he thought the man hiding under the corrugated iron sheet was both a tramp and a German, but not a German tramp, so he could think that Mrs Hayward both was and was not a spy. The concept recalls the earlier comment that the bread knife both was and was not the bayonet, just as the Host both is and is not the body of Christ

 **CHECK THE BOOK**

Spies resembles Ian McEwan's novel *Atonement* (2001) in several respects (see **Background: Literary background**). The passage in which the narrator wonders about understanding events recalls the narrator of *Atonement* (an old woman looking back on events of her childhood) wondering whether events have a meaning.

(Ch. 3, p. 55). Recalling the Host helps to explain Stephen's ability to believe contradictory ideas without any obvious sign of tension – he is required to do it in one sphere (religion), so why should it be difficult in another? By confronting this issue head-on the **narrator** defuses any doubts or disbelief on the part of the reader.

In imagining what the young boy at the window is thinking, the narrator is perhaps attributing to him the type of imaginative projection which so often leads the young Stephen into such fear. However, when he imagines the boy thinking of the dangers he has been warned of, and which the man outside may represent, they are in part **anachronistic**. The old man thinks of terrors from the past and legend, from a mythical earlier England or perhaps his own childhood: 'the pedlars he's been warned against who offer all the terrible pleasures that must be refused, of the torturers of children, of the wandering random murderers' (p. 138). The reference to the 'sick ghosts that haunt the edges of the familiar world' (p. 138) has a mythic quality, even though the narrator may intend the very contemporary threat of paedophiles. The passage has implications, too, for the novel's consideration of the role of the narrator. Throughout, the novel is told by a **first-person narrator** who does not have much insight into even his own earlier **character**. Here, he briefly tries out the role of an **omniscient narrator** who can see into the minds of other characters. He is not very convincing in this, either – his suggestions are pure speculation.

The other important aspect of this chapter is the insight it gives into the dynamics of the cruelty within Keith's family. His father is full of menace, and even while whistling at his work his shadow is intimidating 'like an ogre in his cave' (p. 144). When he speaks to Keith, his thin smile and misappropriated familiarity – 'Come on, old bean' (p. 145) – add a layer of false congeniality that is more sinister than an overt threat would be. Keith knows he is to be punished for something that he has not done, yet neither he nor Stephen can say anything to avert it. Stephen knows what is going on, yet there is a tacit agreement between the two of them that he must always act as though he does not know, and it is a source of embarrassment to them both that he has not gone home before he can witness Keith's pain. Keith is silent during his caning – which

CONTEXT
Acetone (p. 143) is a simple ketone, used in the glue provided with model aeroplane kits and in the dope used to seal wooden and paper models. The paint used for the camouflage of Keith's planes would have been a cellulose paint thinned with acetone. Acetone as a thinner or cleaner in children's model-making has been replaced by safer solvents such as butyl acetate.

leads Stephen to believe there is still time to stop Mr Hayward, though he is impotent to do so. Keith's silence confirms our suspicion that the punishment is a regular occurrence, and also suggests that extra punishment awaits him if he cries out. In running to find Mrs Hayward, Stephen takes decisive action, which is rare for him. He acts bravely, because confronting her with the knowledge shows that he is party to the family's secret, acknowledges that he has been spying on her as he knows where to find her, and breaches the codes of social propriety that bind his life so tightly.

? **QUESTION**

How far is Keith's family, particularly his father, developed in the novel? How does this compare with the development of Stephen's own family?

GLOSSARY

142	**Trossachs** an area of wooded valleys and hills in Scotland. Presumably there is a picture of the Trossachs in the hallway
142	**pagodas** oriental buildings with tiered roofs. Possibly the wallpaper was decorated with a design of pagodas (though this was a feature of 1950s interior design rather than 1930s design) or there was a picture or model of a pagoda in the hall
147	**chassé** a dance step, of which there are many variants, but generally involving three steps in the sequence step-together-step

CHAPTER 8

- Stephen sees nothing of Keith or Mrs Hayward for days.
- Barbara Berrill comes into the hideout one evening, which annoys Stephen. Mrs Hayward approaches but retreats when she sees Barbara; she wanted to ask Stephen to take a letter to the Barns.
- Stephen and some other children trail a policeman from Auntie Dee's house to the Haywards' and speculate about the reason for his visit.
- Barbara visits the hideout again. She and Stephen smoke a cigarette stub they find on the floor.

- Stephen decides that Mrs Hayward is looking after a German airman who has been shot down, and has fallen in love with him.

Stephen watches Keith's house, feels sadly excluded from the more luxurious life he once shared a part of, and is aware without really voicing it that the oppression within is unpleasant. He wonders whether to tell an adult, but can't think who to tell or how to formulate his suspicions. He rejects the idea as tale-telling.

Barbara Berrill comes into the hideout again, and irritates Stephen with her apparent superior knowledge. He feels jealous and is goaded by Barbara's blunt statements – either clumsy or deliberately spiteful – about him no longer being part of Keith's life. The antagonism is brought to a halt when they see Mrs Hayward come out of her gate. They watch as her husband sees her, makes her wait, then accompanies her on her trip to the post box. Stephen realises that Barbara's assessment is right, and Mrs Hayward is closely guarded since coming home inexplicably smeared with slime.

Mrs Hayward makes an excuse to leave her husband, then comes to the hideout intending to get Stephen to take one of her letters. The presence of Barbara makes this impossible, but Barbara has realised what was about to happen.

Another day, Stephen sees children outside Auntie Dee's house and discovers that the policeman is inside investigating another sighting of a reported peeping Tom. The children speculate, and follow the policeman to Keith's house. Again Stephen feels guilty for having done nothing to help Keith's mother.

Barbara again comes to the hideout and tries to engage Stephen in a discussion about the possibility of either Keith's mother or aunt having a boyfriend. Stephen will not be drawn, and instead she talks to him about her sister and his brother, smoking and kissing. Stephen struggles to keep his dignity, pretending to know things he doesn't and to be an experienced smoker. The two of them smoke a cigarette stub they find on the floor.

CONTEXT

Lamorna, the name of Barbara's house (p. 169), is the name of a village on a wild coast in Cornwall, loved by artists. Chollerton (p. 169), after which Keith's house is named, is a more solid and staid village in Northumberland. The names, chosen as much for their sounds as their connotations, mark the different ways Stephen now thinks of these two households.

Barbara makes Stephen open the trunk, and looks at the secret things. Stephen is wracked with guilt and fear at breaking his oath to Keith. Stephen is disturbed by Barbara's weight and softness as she lies across him, and recalls the softness of Mrs Hayward when she collided with him in the tunnel. He is overcome by the cigarette smoke, by burgeoning sexual interest in Barbara and by the heady mixture of guilt, fear and pretending to be grown up.

Stephen sees, in a quick revelation, a new explanation of events, one more in keeping with his new concerns. He imagines that the hidden man is a German airman shot down in a raid and that Keith's mother and aunt have been looking after him in honour of Uncle Peter, and that Mrs Hayward has become attracted to him and 'take[n] him to her bosom' (p. 170).

The chapter ends with Mrs Hayward approaching to ask Stephen the question he has been dreading – whether he will take a letter for her.

COMMENTARY

The chapter starts with a **rhetorical question**, 'What's going to happen now?' This voices a question readers may ask themselves. It underlines Frayn's **conceit** of not knowing how the action will turn out, as his **narrator** struggles to reconstruct events from his memory. At the same time, it is a question the younger Stephen is asking himself. This time, the interruption by the voice of the older narrator draws us back from the action in the past for only a moment, as the question smoothly becomes Stephen's.

Stephen cannot resolve his desire to tell an adult about what might be going on into any definite action. He is aware that he can't say exactly what is happening, and that whatever he says is likely to be dismissed as childish meddling. This throws him back on the schoolboy's moral code in which telling tales is always wrong. He questions this: 'So telling tales is worse than spying? Worse than letting someone put the lives of our soldiers and sailors at risk?' (p. 152). This struggle with his status and moral code as a child is balanced by the closing part of the chapter in which he feels he is moving away from childhood and approaching deeper, adult mysteries.

> **CONTEXT**
>
> Stephen's phraseology, 'put the lives of our soldiers and sailors at risk' (p. 152), recalls war propaganda about the dangers posed by 'careless talk' and other risks to national security. He has internalised these government warnings, but they are unexamined and undigested, surfacing in their original wording to produce a comic disjunction.

The two interludes with Barbara Berrill mark the beginning of Stephen's emergence from childhood. He is vulnerable to her because he 'feel[s] too miserable even to tell her to go away' (p. 153) – or so he tells himself. He lets her stay, though she annoys him with her apparent knowledge of what is going on at Keith's house, and he thinks that she is deliberately goading him. However, from thinking her stupid, he agrees that she is right in her interpretation of Mr Hayward's desire to accompany his wife to the post box. Barbara now has some slight hold over Stephen as he has admitted she was right in one regard and she has seen something of his relationship with Mrs Hayward.

On Barbara's second visit, Stephen is keen not to look immature or foolish in front of her. In sharing a cigarette with her he attempts to seem grown up and worldly wise. She is impressed by his ability to smoke and this encourages him to engage more with her. It also makes him vulnerable. When she lies across him and demands the key to the trunk he is unable to resist. Conflicting emotions in Stephen surface one after another, making a gentle comedy. His characteristic, uptight childish obsession with germs – '"You'll get germs!" I cry, shocked' (p. 164) – gives way to sharing the cigarette in an attempt to look sophisticated. His anxiety about Keith and the oath is still present and surfaces when Barbara comments on the 'bayonet'. But Stephen acknowledges that it looks like a carving knife to him, too (p. 165), as Keith is starting to lose his hold over him.

Stephen here considers himself on the brink of growing up, leaving behind the fantasy games he has played with Keith and embarking on new, more adult mysteries. The softness of Barbara's body lying across him, and memories of Mrs Hayward's soft bosom in the tunnel, start the first stirrings of sexual interest in Stephen. His feeling of vertigo, created by these feelings and his guilt at violating the secrecy he shares with Keith, leads to his new perception of evenings in the Close. The name of Barbara's house, which is significantly opposite Keith's house, reverberates in his head. It seems to contain and explain all his new feelings, experiences and insights and to embody a wildness and a wealth of new possibilities not accessible to him before. The names of the two houses, both

CONTEXT

Stephen spells 'Shnick-shnack' (p. 152) as it sounds because as a boy he does not know the word's origin. When he talks of using the same word to his own children at the end of the novel, he gives the correct German spelling 'Schnickschnack' (Ch. 11, p. 231).

place names like the Sorrentos and Windermeres referred to earlier, come to stand for different ways of life and different paths he can take. Keith's house, stolidly middle-class, clean and oppressive, is on one side of the street. Barbara's house, redolent of chaos, wildness, new experiences and freedom, stands facing it. In choosing Barbara, he has to deny Keith. In seeing the bayonet as a carving knife, he shows that he is ready to do so.

CHAPTER 9

- With effort, Mrs Hayward persuades Stephen to take a basket of provisions and a letter to the man in hiding.
- Barbara Berrill comes into the hideout before Stephen has had time to go on his errand. They smoke, and she kisses him, and then insists on seeing the things in the basket. They fight when she opens the sealed letter.
- Mr Hayward calls Stephen out of the hideout and makes him surrender the basket.
- Distraught by all that has happened, Stephen suffers nightmares. He takes supplies from his own house and goes to the Barns. As he approaches, a voice from under the corrugated iron sheet speaks his name.

Mrs Hayward comes into the hideout with a basket which she wants Stephen to take to the man in hiding. Stephen is embarrassed, for himself and for her, at her having to abase herself to this degree – to come into his hideout, to ask a difficult favour of a child, to put him in the awkward position of having power over her. As usual, confusion makes him dumb, and he can't even articulate by shaking or nodding his head. She becomes increasingly distressed, and her tears horrify him. Unable to get away, he just looks at the ground and waits for his ordeal to be over. In the end, she gives up and asks him to keep her secret but, as she stands to leave, he takes the basket from her, agreeing to deliver it. Mr Hayward has twice been out to the gate to look for his wife. Stephen knows she will be in trouble for being away.

After Mrs Hayward has gone, Barbara comes to the hideout and sees the basket. She tries to persuade Stephen to share its secret with her, and when he refuses she becomes mean and unpleasant. Stephen finds the change from her new self back to her old persona unbearable and finally turns on her, reminding her that they were going to be friends. She softens, and they share a cigarette she has smuggled. United again, they take the things out of the basket together. Barbara kisses Stephen, which surprises him. Despite Stephen's struggles, she sits on top of him and opens the letter from the basket. They are discovered by Mr Hayward, who makes Stephen follow him to his garage, with the basket. Stephen is completely disarmed when Mr Hayward asks politely for the basket, and he hands it over. Mrs Hayward comes in and sees what has happened, but fails to recover the situation and sends Stephen out.

Stephen is extremely upset, but cannot explain why to his parents. He has terrible dreams and realises with horror that one day he will be dead. The next day, he takes supplies from his own house and makes his way to the Barns. With great difficulty, he conquers his fear of the children in the Lanes and of the dogs and even of the man in hiding. As he puts the supplies on the top step and turns to go, a voice from within says his name.

COMMENTARY

The narratorial point of view changes again as the **narrator** tries to remember exactly what happened. This has the effect of distancing us from the action, disturbing the **dramatic tension** created at the end of the last chapter as we anticipate Stephen's difficult meeting with Mrs Hayward, and reinforcing the idea that there is somewhere a true sequence of events that he could possibly uncover from his memory. Stephen is referred to in the third person and the action is narrated in the past tense. Part way down page 177, though, we are thrown back into the present of the war. Stephen is again a **first-person narrator** and he tells events in the present tense. The drama is allowed to resume, the tension to build, and all uncertainty is expunged from the narrative. From being unsure of what was said and the sequence of events, the narrator has switched to giving reported speech and tiny details of description and action.

> **CONTEXT**
>
> As at the end of many chapters, the **narrative** ends with a cliffhanger, encouraging us to read on. This recalls the episodes of adventure stories published in boys' magazines of the 1940s in which each week the story ended at a point of impending crisis, encouraging the reader to buy the next issue. There is more about the relation of *Spies* to boys' adventure stories in **Background: Literary background**.

Stephen's intense awareness of his own responsibility is emphasised throughout this chapter. He sees it as entirely his own fault that Mrs Hayward can no longer make her trips to the tunnel, entirely his fault that Barbara has invaded the secret hideout, and finally that whatever awful punishment awaits Mrs Hayward at the hands of her husband is also his fault. While he bears some responsibility, he is certainly not the only culpable character in any of these instances. His tendency to excessive self-blame is characteristic of a child who is always feeling chastised (as Stephen is by Keith), and who develops a poor self-image. It is a more general human characteristic, when we are feeling guilty about something, to assume a greater share of the guilt than other people might assign to us. In this, Stephen's behaviour is entirely recognisable. His fear, which leads to his nightmares, is similarly familiar and we **empathise** with him. He endures the terrible, inevitable realisation that comes to all children sooner or later that 'there will come a day when I'm dead, and from that day forth I shall be dead for ever' (p. 193). Though the thought surfaces at this moment because of his fears for the man living (or dying) underground, the realisation is a part of the growing-up process that is shown, too, in his burgeoning feelings towards Barbara.

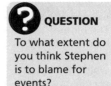

QUESTION

To what extent do you think Stephen is to blame for events?

Stephen's sexual awakenings, begun in the previous chapter, continue in this meeting with Barbara. He is distressed that at first she seems to have reverted to her earlier spiteful behaviour, and he is desperate to regain what they had achieved. The change in his attitude towards her is signalled in his response to her blue purse, which had previously been a focus of his derision. Now, 'The popper opens and closes with a sweetly satisfying sound, I notice, as if it were saying "Lamorna" as a single syllable' (p. 184). 'Lamorna' has come to stand for everything sweet, chaotic and full of promise that he associates with Barbara.

The interlude with Barbara is brought to a sudden conclusion by the appearance of Mr Hayward. What he interrupts, as Barbara sits astride Stephen and he yells out his objections, must look very like an inverted rape scene. After kissing him, Barbara has thrown Stephen to the ground and is pinning him down while he shouts 'No! ... Don't! We mustn't!' (p. 186), but Mr Hayward appears completely oblivious to whatever they may be doing. 'Can I have a word with you, old chap?' (p. 186), he says, his faux-congeniality full of menace. The **narrator** comments on his familiarity: 'he called me "old chap", almost as if I were one of the family' (p. 187). There are sinister undertones to this, since being one of Mr Hayward's family means being subject to his regime of bullying and torture.

Stephen's exchange with Mr Hayward reveals more about both **characters** and also brings Stephen the surprising discovery that there is some form of kinship between adults and children – they are not completely different species as he had always assumed. Even as he is terrified of Mr Hayward he notices the man's awkwardness and uncertainty – Stephen is not part of his family, and he is unsure how to dominate him. Although he is finally undone by Mr Hayward's polite request, Stephen demonstrates a new bravery in this scene. For as long as Mr Hayward uses the chilling false levity and familiarity beneath which he habitually hides his now all too apparent abusive behaviour, Stephen has an idea of how to cope. He knows that Mr Hayward can't touch him, as he is someone else's child and propriety does not allow him to hurt Stephen. But he is disarmed by Mr Hayward's 'Please' (p. 189), for now propriety demands that he comply with the adult's request.

Stephen's distress during the night underlines his childishness. Again he is inarticulate, unable to tell his parents about his troubles, and he reverts to a child's response to his anxiety by crawling into his parents' bed. But as his anxiety turns to resolve, he is brave again in the morning. He acts heroically in going to the Barns: he conquers his fears in order to do what he feels is right, and what he believes he is compelled to do. His terror, which he sees as evidence of cowardice, is instead evidence of bravery – he is terrified, yet still does what he feels he should do. As readers, we admire him, although there is nothing in the text to direct us explicitly towards this admiration. The presentation of Stephen's journey to the Barns recreates in us his unwillingness to go on, the sense of the journey extending endlessly towards a conclusion better avoided.

The chapter ends with a shock, as much to us as to Stephen, when the man in the 'living grave' (p. 195) speaks his name. With a lurch, the entire tenor of the adventure has changed. Once more, a simple phrase has changed everything. The word recalls the end of the previous chapter, when Mrs Hayward approached Stephen in his own hiding place and spoke his name. In this symmetry, Uncle Peter and Mrs Hayward are set in the same relation to Stephen, and his role as a go-between is underscored by the structure of the narrative.

GLOSSARY

195   expiating   making amends for

CHAPTER 10

- Stephen is forced to listen to the man underground but gives little response himself.
- He agrees to carry a token, a silk scarf, to Mrs Hayward and to give her a message.
- He finds the scarf is a map of the German countryside. He takes it to the privet hedge to hide. He is discovered by Keith.
- Keith wounds Stephen's throat with the bread knife because he believes Stephen has broken his oath. Stephen does not surrender the silk scarf.
- In the night, Stephen goes to the railway embankment to hide the scarf. He finds the place full of men clearing a dead body from the track in front of a waiting train.

Stephen is disturbed that the person hiding underground knows his name. Reluctantly, he answers some of the man's questions, though he avoids as many as he can. Stephen's unresponsiveness leads the man to reveal more of himself. He asks about Auntie Dee and Milly, as well as Bobs – the use of Mrs Hayward's first name (p. 200) shocks Stephen – and he finally reveals his own history. Likening Stephen's game that has got out of hand to his own situation he tells how he lost his nerve flying and can no longer even pretend to be

CONTEXT

Pilots were often issued with silk maps of Germany during the Second World War. The map would help them find their way to the border and evade capture if they were shot down over enemy territory.

brave. Stephen stands dumbly by. Eventually, the man gives Stephen the silk scarf from his neck. He is unable to write a note for Bobs, but tells Stephen to give her the simple message 'For ever'. This becomes the latest in a string of words and phrases that resonate in Stephen's mind.

Back at home, Stephen looks at the scarf and discovers that it is a map of Germany. He wonders how to get it to Mrs Hayward, and decides to hide the scarf in the chest in the hideout.

The hideout is different, and it is clear that Barbara Berrill has been to it and tidied it up. She has corrected the spelling on the tile, too, to 'Private'. It is no longer Keith's space. From the hideout, Stephen sees that Auntie Dee is visiting Mrs Hayward. He has never seen this before. There is obviously something wrong, as Millie is crying in her pushchair and he sees Auntie Dee and Mrs Hayward distressed and anxious.

Finally, Keith comes to the hideout. Keith decides that Stephen has shown their secret things to Barbara, and makes him swear that he has not. He doesn't believe him, though, and wounds Stephen's throat with the bread knife kept in the chest. Stephen manages to withhold the scarf from Keith, even though he senses that it is all that will stop Keith hurting him.

Stephen returns home, where he tries to hide his injury. His mother notices, though, and his parents are both caring and solicitous as they dress his wound and try desperately to discover who has hurt him. But Stephen will not speak.

In the night, Stephen wakes to hear a strange hissing sound. He goes to the railway to hide the scarf but finds that the area is different in the darkness. Soon it becomes clear that there are people there, with a truck. A train has stopped on the tracks, and that is the source of the hissing sound. Stephen hides and watches as the men recover the body of the man from the Barns (Uncle Peter) from the railway track, though Stephen does not see the corpse. Stephen imagines that the man was electrocuted by the live rail and then run over by a train.

CONTEXT

Pushchairs in the 1940s did not have complex integral straps like modern pushchairs, but sometimes had a single strap or were used with a separate baby harness. Often, a pram was adapted to a pushchair by folding down the end at the baby's feet. The baby always faced the parent, unlike modern pushchairs in which the baby often faces forward.

COMMENTARY

This chapter is packed with incidents. The **narrative** rushes towards its conclusion in sharp contrast with the slow pace of the earlier part of the novel. In a single chapter, Stephen is forced to talk to the man hiding at the Barns, to confront Keith and be punished for sharing secrets with Barbara, and to discover that the man at the Barns is now dead. Stephen's **character** is explored further in these times of tension and testing, and we learn more, too, about Keith and his home life.

As before, Stephen is unable to speak in his encounter with the man at the Barns. The older **narrator** is not able to say whether at this point he realised the true identity of the man, and recognised him as Keith's Uncle Peter. The narrator steps back from the action for a moment to say that he is unsure whether, as a child, he recognised the voice and understood finally who it was. He seems still to hold the ideas of his being a tramp and being German in tension, and to persist despite the man clearly being English and knowing him: 'I think he still thought the man was an old tramp, but perhaps now he realised that he was also not an old tramp … he was beginning to understand that he was a German who was entirely English' (p. 200). For Stephen, being a tramp or a German has come to stand for something other than its literal meaning. The man is alien, unlike Stephen: dirty (Germ-man), and an enemy in some way.

Stephen's inability to answer questions, while frustrating to the pilot, also clears a path for him to deliver a monologue in which we discover what happened to him, how he deserted the Air Force and has no choice but to hide until the end of the war. He, too, refers to the activities of Stephen and Keith as a game – a game that has got out of hand. With sad **irony**, he likens their game to his own naive excitement at being able to play the part of a war hero and fighter pilot, and describes how he became tired at playing at being brave. His use of the second person, 'You're up there in the darkness five hundred miles from home and suddenly the darkness is inside you as well' (p. 203), helps Uncle Peter to distance the account from himself by making it someone else's experience. He is saying 'you' to Stephen, when he has just been talking of Stephen's game-

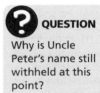

QUESTION

Why is Uncle Peter's name still withheld at this point?

playing: 'You start playing some game' (p. 203). We recognise in the terror he describes an echo of the terror that is now plaguing Stephen. This helps to reinforce the bond between his own 'game' of war and Stephen's game of spying.

In addition, it speaks to us as readers – we too are asked to imagine ourselves in his place, flying a plane in the dark and terrified of death. If we might have condemned him for his cowardice, we cannot after this as we are implicated, put in the same position, forced to take the same involuntary action. There is no space in which to criticise this **character**. It is clear now that the man is Keith's Uncle Peter, Auntie Dee's heroic husband, but his name is still not revealed. Uncle Peter's terror and consequent failure in his duty are givens that cannot be examined. The moral questions of the novel do not involve what he did or failed to do, but how the other characters in the novel have dealt with what happens and the consequences that have arisen from it.

Continuing a longstanding trend in the novel, the revelation that Uncle Peter has always been in love with Bobs rather than his wife, Auntie Dee, is presented almost as an aside (p. 205). We are never allowed to know whether he has been having an affair with Mrs Hayward, or whether his feelings for her are reciprocated. Ironically, Stephen's childish conclusion that she had 'take[n] him to her bosom' (Ch. 8, p. 170) is not so far from the truth, though he had no evidence on which to base his guess.

Although Stephen constantly undermines himself, we are likely to judge him more kindly than he does himself. His actions are often brave; he conquers his fear of the man at the Barns to take him supplies. He talks to him when he would rather run away. It is not clear that he really would take the man's water bucket and flee as he suggests – it seems more likely that his sense of duty would compel him to refill and return it. He is desperate to get away, but unable to move, held there by the authority of a grown-up telling him what to do and wanting to talk to him. Even though the man is sick and hidden and could not compel Stephen physically, Stephen is incapable of ignoring his innate authority as an adult. He stands up to Keith's terrible treatment of him and abides by his (misguided) code of honour in refusing to reveal to his parents what has happened to him. His code is entirely internalised and cannot be challenged: 'I don't show him the scarf, because it can't be shown. I don't say the words, because they can't be said' (p. 209). Stephen goes out into the night to hide the scarf when he cannot see how to give it to Mrs Hayward. Though he knows this is the wrong course to take, he is afraid the scarf will be discovered and overcomes his terror in order to hide it.

Stephen's habit of blaming himself for everything continues as he, inevitably, blames himself first for what he suspects is someone coming to look for the man and then for the man's death on the railway. He has a childish belief in some form of universal justice, in which what occurs is as a result of his own actions being rewarded or punished: 'They're coming for him because I let myself be bullied once again' (p. 209). Like many bullied children, he blames himself for his own mistreatment.

As with every encounter with Uncle Peter, this crucial action takes place in the darkness and is barely seen. When Stephen is disturbed by Uncle Peter at the metal box by the railway, he doesn't see the man; no one can identify the man Auntie Dee is seen kissing, nor the peeping Tom, and during Stephen's long talk with Uncle Peter at the Barns the man is hard to make out, hidden in the gloom under ground. Stephen is in hiding, watching men move around in the dark. He does not see the body of Uncle Peter. We know that it is disfigured because one of the stretcher bearers – presumably used to gruesome sights – is sick after looking at what is left of him. The mangled remains of a Spitfire on the waiting train go unremarked upon, but are a silent reminder of the fate that Uncle Peter feared and sought to avoid.

> **CONTEXT**
>
> The place names on the map – Chemnitz, Leipzig and Zwickau (p. 211) – are three towns close together in a small area of Saxony, eastern Germany, and close to the border with the Czech Republic (as it is now). Chemnitz and Leipzig were heavily bombed by the Allied forces. Zwickau survived largely unscathed. It was the site of a large concentration camp.

> **CONTEXT**
>
> Ena Harkness (p. 208) is the name of a rose. It is a climbing hybrid tea rose with large, double, bright crimson flowers and a sweet scent.

> **GLOSSARY**
>
> 203   **dicky** not working properly

CHAPTER 11

- The narrator reviews the Close and the surrounding area and wonders what has become of the silk scarf.
- He fills in brief details of the rest of his childhood and what happened to some of the characters.
- The narrator reveals that his family was German-Jewish, and that later in life he returned to Germany and assumed again his German name, Stefan Weitzler.
- He reflects on when he realised that Keith's Uncle Peter was the man at the Barns, and again feels disoriented and slightly homesick as he turns to leave the Close.

The older Stephen is aware that he has been walking around the neighbourhood for long enough to look suspicious. He goes to the railway embankment for a final time, but there, too, everything has changed and he cannot get near the place where he hid the silk map. He returns to the past to fill in details, telling us that life continued in much the same way except that he didn't speak to Keith, who was sent went away to boarding school. Uncle Peter was reported missing, Auntie Dee fell out with her sister and moved away, and Barbara turned her attentions to Dave Avery, giving Stephen his first experience of disappointment in love.

In a complete change of direction, the **narrator** reveals that he was the German spy in the Close. On a first reading of the novel, this revelation is likely to come as a surprise as the hints that he is German have been subtle and easily missed. He explains that he was young when his family left Germany in 1935 and only learned German in his adolescence. He was dissatisfied with his humdrum life and marriage in England and, after the deaths of his parents in 1960 and 1961, he returned to Germany. He discovered that his first home had been similar to the Close in London. He struggled for a while, but stayed in Germany. He discovered that most of his father's family had been killed by the Nazis, but that his sister (Stephen's aunt) and her children had died in a bombing raid by the RAF. Stephen (now Stefan) stayed in Germany, working as a technical translator; he re-married and had children. Now his children are grown up and his wife has died.

His father had helped other German refugees during the war, and had been called back from internment in the Isle of Man because his technical expertise was needed by British military intelligence. Stephen's idle boast to Keith that his father was a German spy **ironically** held some truth – he was German, and a spy of sorts, though not a spy for Germany. Stephen's brother, Geoff, stayed in England and has since died of lung cancer.

Stephen wonders about the other inhabitants of the street. He believes Keith has become a barrister, and imagines for a moment that the elderly woman he sees at Number 6 is Barbara, but then dismisses this as fancy.

He wonders when he realised that the man at the Barns was Uncle Peter, and this leads him to wondering when Uncle Peter realised that it was Bobs he loved and not Auntie Dee. He thinks for a moment about the English and Germans in the war – their equivalent terror and deaths – and wonders where his home is. The novel ends with him noticing again the scent of privet that brought him here.

COMMENTARY

There are many major life events and tragic episodes crammed into Stephen's summing-up of his life, most of which go completely unexamined. This gives a sense of other stories that could be told, and invites us to reflect on how the brief episode in his childhood that the novel has explored may have had an impact on later events. As usual, Stephen does not offer any commentary or interpretation. He reports traumatic events in an even and unemotional tone and again avoids saying things directly. We learn that his wife has died because he says he and his children 'have their mother's grave to tend each week' (p. 230). Even in referring to her as 'their mother' he creates distance between himself and his dead wife. Perhaps he is being careful not to invite sympathy, but the tendency to remove himself from the immediacy of events has persisted throughout the novel.

> **CONTEXT**
>
> During both the First and Second World Wars, Germans resident in Britain were sent away to internment camps, some of which were on the Isle of Man, an independent realm in the Irish Sea. By 1940, there were 14,000 'enemy aliens' in prison camps on the island.

> **CONTEXT**
>
> The Inner Temple (p. 232) is one of the four Inns of Court where judges and barristers train and work in central London. The name 'Temple' comes from the order of the Knights Templar, who founded a church on the site in the mid-twelfth century.

CHECK THE NET
For an account of the role of Bomber Command in the Second World War, see the RAF website **www.rafbomber command.com**

CONTEXT
Stephen recalls being called a 'sheeny' (Ch. 4, p. 64) at school. This is a disparaging term for a Jew, and is the first hint that his family is Jewish. Although the persecution of Jewish people during the Second World War was deprecated by the Allies, there was little sympathy for Jews among the British population. Prejudice and racism against Jewish children would have been unremarkable and would usually go unpunished in British schools at the time.

The war, which has been present as background through the main part of the story, is given more prominence in this chapter than anywhere else. The clash between the Germans and the English, which has been held at arm's length while Stephen's Germanness was unacknowledged, comes to the fore when we learn of the death in a bombing raid of Stephen's aunt in Germany who was 'killed in her own cellar, along with her two children, by Uncle Peter, or by his colleagues in Bomber Command' (p. 229). The order of the sentence makes it impossible not to think, for a moment, that Uncle Peter himself killed Stephen's relatives. It immediately puts Uncle Peter's experience in quite a different light. The idea is revisited at the very end when Uncle Peter's terror in the sky and Stephen's aunt's imagined terror in her cellar are juxtaposed. Both are victims, ordinary English people and ordinary German people. Frayn is an English novelist, writing predominantly for a British audience. He elicits a more thoughtful response from his readers by having German civilians killed by a British bomber than he would if it were the other way round. Our sympathy is with the bombed woman and children and with all innocent civilians, regardless of nationality.

Stephen reveals that his family is Jewish and that his parents kept his heritage secret from him (as he has kept it secret from us). His brother, too, did not tell Stephen where they had come from. He supposes this was intended to make life easier for him – he would probably have been bullied even more if his background was known. But it has probably contributed to the rootless feeling that Stephen now has, of not knowing where he belongs and of 'which is here and which is there' (p. 230). He is caught between two cultures, and has made his career out of this dislocation by becoming a translator.

The material Stephen translates is made to sound as dull as possible. Technical manuals on the installation and maintenance of transformers and switching gear will not appeal to many people, but even so he further undermines it with a negative introduction, 'I don't suppose you've ever read' (p. 229). This is the only time he ever addresses the reader as 'you'. Its impact is to draw us in, as though he is sharing something with just us, individually. It is the

only time there is a suggestion that the story is told for anyone other than himself.

This final chapter has the status of an **epilogue** or **codicil**. The story is over, with the 'game' (Ch. 10, p. 222) at the end of the previous chapter. Here, we might expect loose ends to be tied up. But they are not. More loose ends are suggested. What became of the other **characters**? What is the true tale of the love between Bobs and Uncle Peter? All mysteries, he says, have been 'as resolved as they're ever likely to be' (p. 234) – which is not very resolved at all. We are left wondering, for he does not tell us, whether the **narrator** has found any satisfaction in his journey back into his past. He is still feeling the strange combination of longing for home and for elsewhere, of *Heimweh* and *Fernweh*. As he says right at the start of the novel, 'I have a kind of homesickness for where I am' (Ch. 1, p. 3). He is no closer to knowing where his home lies, except in the past which he can never regain.

> **CONTEXT**
>
> The need to decrypt German messages during the war hastened the development of computers. The first programmable computer was built at Bletchley Park in 1943 to crack German codes. The computer was destroyed after the war.

> **GLOSSARY**
>
> 230   **decrypts** Messages sent in encrypted form by German military and intercepted and deciphered by Allied military intelligence. When the content of the message was highly technical, independent experts were sometimes needed to explain it

EXTENDED COMMENTARIES

TEXT 1 – CHAPTER 8, PAGES 154–5

From *'Barbara Berrill puts her hand over her mouth ...'* to *'... small point of domestic routine.'*

Barbara Berrill has crept into the hideout while Stephen is sitting there miserably reflecting. Keith has been caned for taking the thermos flask and Stephen has taken the initiative and communicated the disaster to Mrs Hayward. Stephen has been wondering whether he can tell someone about Mrs Hayward's spying.

In a humiliatingly easy leap of imagination, Barbara suggests that perhaps 'Mrs Hayward's got a boyfriend, too, like Mrs Tracey' and that her husband has found out. In this simple, throw-away remark, Barbara has solved the mystery which has exercised Stephen and Keith for so long, though none of the characters knows she has. For Barbara, it is of no importance whether her guess is correct – she is amusing herself and trying to embarrass Stephen by playing with the possibility. For Stephen, ironically, the suggestion is ridiculous. Only we as readers are likely to see that in all probability she has hit on the correct interpretation. An additional **irony** is that the boyfriend in question is not just 'like' Mrs Tracey's boyfriend, but *is* Mrs Tracey's 'boyfriend'.

The **narrator**'s humour is directed against Stephen as he voices Stephen's thoughts in response to Barbara's suggestion: 'I know perfectly well that this is just a further example of the stupid things that girls say'. Barbara is more worldly-wise than Stephen. Further, she has a girl's interest in and instinct for social and emotional matters that mean nothing to Stephen. For Stephen, the suggestion that Mrs Hayward's secret might be something as dully domestic and ordinary as an affair is not only absurd, but also disappointing. In his world of boys' adventures such a domestic intrigue would not warrant any attention.

In this passage, Stephen is presented in the first person. As usual, though, the narratorial voice is not quite Stephen's but is used to convey Stefan's ideas and judgement of himself as he looks back. He recognises jealousy in his response, but is not sure whether he is jealous of Barbara's assumed insight into Keith's situation, or jealous of Keith's role as his mother's helper in her secret, or whether he is jealous of Mrs Hayward's supposed boyfriend. The last of these is very much an interpretation offered by the adult Stefan as Stephen would be horrified at any suggestion that he has a romantic interest in Mrs Hayward. Through the narrator's agency, we are able to watch his attraction towards her develop, but the boy is completely unaware of it.

Barbara changes tack, offering to adopt Stephen's method of investigation by suggesting they follow Keith. Whether this is

prompted just by her curiosity or whether she hopes to appease Stephen is unclear. But Stephen is far from appeased. Rather, he feels she is encroaching on his territory, hijacking the boys' adventure and trying to supplant Keith. Worse, Keith is to become the object of their spying. His outrage is communicated by the use of two exclamation marks and the indignant 'actually' to underline the ridiculousness of the suggestion.

In the following paragraphs, Barbara's powers of deduction are set against Stephen's as they both interpret the scene unfolding before them and come to very different initial conclusions. Stephen sees Mrs Hayward close the door 'very gently'; Barbara sees her being furtive – 'She's creeping out'. Stephen assumes since she is holding letters that she is still allowed to go to the post box. It doesn't occur to him that she is going furtively. This disingenuousness is rather endearing. It is thrown into sharp relief by Barbara's more astute assessment of the situation as it continues. Barbara, with a note of drama, whispers 'Oh no!' She is engaged with the situation, identifying with Mrs Hayward and feeling for her when her plan to sneak out is foiled. Beside her, Stephen observes dispassionately, itemising the actions of Mrs and then Mr Hayward. When he attempts to interpret what he sees, he is an unreliable witness. Mrs Hayward is, he says 'tranquil and unhurried'. She may be unhurried, but we doubt she is tranquil. While Barbara can see immediately that the couple disagree when they talk, Stephen obstinately or naively refuses to acknowledge it: 'So far as I can see, they are talking quietly and reasonably'. Because they are not shouting, gesticulating or looking confrontational, Stephen cannot detect any conflict. It takes Barbara's female eye and enthusiasm for emotional engagement to discern the tension between the two.

QUESTION

How much do we learn about Stephen from the counterpointing of Stephen and Barbara Berrill in the various scenes in the hideout?

Stephen is probably aware that he is deceiving himself. He refers to them settling 'some small point of domestic routine' but he knows that there is far more than this wrong in the Hayward household. On the page following this extract, he finally has to admit that Barbara's interpretation is correct and give up his refusal to see it: '"Barbara Berrill's right", he says' (p. 156), admitting that he knows the slime on Mrs Hayward's dress has, like a badge, advertised what

she is doing secretly and that now 'Keith's Daddy … won't let her set foot outside the house'.

TEXT 2 – CHAPTER 9, PAGES 187–8

From 'The light's on above the workbench …' to 'And I won't.'

This passage is Stephen's only personal encounter with Mr Hayward. Throughout the novel, Mr Hayward ignores Stephen completely, speaking only to Keith when he encounters the two boys together. Of Uncle Peter, the **narrator** says, 'His very absence was a kind of presence' (p. 25), but with Mr Hayward, his presence is a kind of absence.

The garage is Mr Hayward's domain. Stephen has not been into it before, though he has seen Mr Hayward working in there and has found its smell alluring. Now the garage is immediately full of menace. Mr Hayward has something small 'held in the jaws of the great vice'. This is to be Stephen's position soon, and he knows it – he will be the small thing that is held immobile and unable to escape while Mr Hayward works on him. The 'jaws' of the vice create a fleeting image of a great monster about to eat the small thing and we recall an earlier image of Mr Hayward, 'like an ogre in his cave' (p. 144). The smell of the garage, which has been mentioned with the same enumeration of components twice before, now has the addition of fear. This is because Stephen is now in the garage – he's brought the smell of fear with him.

In the blank line between Mr Hayward leading Stephen in to the garage and the first paragraph in this passage, Mr Hayward has returned to his workbench and resumed working and whistling. This might seem a strange thing to do as he has brought Stephen into the garage to talk to him, but it works by making Stephen feel awkward, out of place and ignored. As soon as Mr Hayward speaks, the level of tension rises further. He uses the false congeniality that is his trademark, and the truncated syntax, 'quick and dry and impatient' (p. 22), that makes all his speech into commands. His first words would, in another context, sound as though they were offered in a friendly vein: 'Word of advice, old fellow'. However, we known that this air of congeniality always cloaks his brutality and it

is immediately more chilling than if he were openly angry. As he adjusts the micrometer on his piece of metal, we know that he will be trying out different methods of extracting the information and the basket from Stephen, and is judging how to do it.

In these few paragraphs, he is more voluble than he has ever been. For once, he speaks in whole sentences. His speech is packed with **idioms** of the 1940s: 'awful asses', 'let's-pretend', 'old chap'. It appears that he finds speech rather difficult, that his language is a patchwork of well worn phrases, appropriated to serve a sinister purpose.

Mr Hayward seems to share his wife's poor judgement of their son's character as he says that he doesn't want ideas put into Keith's head. He, too, assumes that Stephen is leading the 'silly games'. But when he says that he has 'had a word with Keith' we can be certain that this means he has punished him, and it raises the level of anxiety for Stephen still further.

When Mr Hayward smiles his awful thin smile, that is always a prelude to violence, it looks different to Stephen and he realises with surprise that Mr Hayward is finding this interview awkward. He cannot use his usual tactics, as Stephen is not his son. A new insight opens up for Stephen, that grown-ups are not completely different after all. This is a momentary distraction from the torment of the moment, and is presented with slight humour: 'Even Keith's father belongs to a branch of the animal kingdom that has some kinship with my own'. The narrator's voice speaks in longer, eloquent sentences with an urbane sense of humour that is in complete contrast with Mr Hayward's inarticulate fragments. We are taken out of the moment briefly as Stephen takes another step towards maturity with this realisation. But we are returned to the scene quickly, and Mr Hayward is clearly succeeding in dominating Stephen as even his own words now follow the pattern of short sentences: 'I nod again. There's nothing else I can do', 'The basket. We've got there. ... Silence. ... I go on looking at the floor'. Looking at the floor releases Stephen from Mr Hayward's spell again and his own voice returns. This paragraph is a beautiful evocation of how we can distract ourselves from something

> **CONTEXT**
>
> A micrometer is an instrument used in mechanical engineering for measuring very small distances. The type of micrometer Keith's father is using here is probably an external micrometer. Rather like callipers with gradations marked on a scale, an external micrometer is used to measure the width of a block or wire.

> **CONTEXT**
>
> Characters in the novels of Evelyn Waugh (1903–66) speak the same language as Mr Hayward, though with more articulacy. Their speech is similarly peppered with 'old chap' and 'old girl', but to completely different effect.

unpleasant by concentrating on an irrelevant and insignificant detail. It recreates the way that time moves slowly in moments of crisis, too. In the space between Mr Hayward's words, Stephen is able to observe the floor minutely, find something interesting in it and speculate. The image of the pebbles that have 'somehow freed themselves and disappeared' we see as a wistful longing on his part that he could somehow free himself and disappear from this terrible situation and from his position on the floor of the garage. But Mr Hayward breaks back in through Stephen's reverie with his demand.

Stephen's spirit is not broken, however. He continues his dreams of respite, this time imagining hermit crabs taking refuge. Even when Mr Hayward uses his most frightening phrase, 'old bean', that always presages physical punishment for Keith, Stephen stands his ground and has another insight, this time into the surprising impotence of Mr Hayward in this situation. Again the gentle humour that comes from his eloquent and accomplished choice of words asserts Stephen's power 'by some improbable stroke of kindly providence he's not my father'. In the final sentence of this passage, Stephen is defiant, resolute and triumphant (though it turns out to be only briefly so). In his three-word paragraph, he even turns Mr Hayward's abrupt syntax against him: 'And I won't.'

> **CONTEXT**
>
> Hermit crabs have a hard shell only on the front part of their body. The back part is pulpy and soft. To protect itself, the hermit crab inhabits a discarded shell (from a shellfish rather than a snail). As it grows, it needs to find a larger shell. It is vulnerable while it scuttles from one shell to the next.

TEXT 3 – CHAPTER 10, PAGE 203

From '"Poor kid" …' to '… I have to wait.'

Stephen has listened for a long time to the man at the Barns. He has not yet realised (or admitted to himself) that the man is Uncle Peter.

The speaker begins by addressing Stephen directly, 'Poor kid'. As he begins to talk he slides from talking about Stephen to speaking about himself, yet he continues to use the second person. At first, he refers to the game that Stephen and Keith have been playing, but he opens it up to make it a general and habitual situation, with 'that's what happens'. As he says 'You start playing some game', the word 'some' is both dismissive and helps to generalise – it doesn't matter what the game is, the process is the same. We realise that for him the game was war, and being a war hero.

The monotonous repetition of 'goes on and on … gets more and more frightening' extends the sentence like Uncle Peter's experience was extended; we feel it stretching ahead. And then the particular replaces the general, with 'one night'. Suddenly there is **dramatic tension** – 'it happens'. What happens? From trailing along slowly with the last sentence, we suddenly feel the tension and want to rush on and find out what happens. He sets the dramatic scene, five hundred miles from home, in the sky, in darkness. The use of 'you' makes the ensuing description of how he felt very immediate and vivid. It is recreated in our imaginations as our own feeling, and very physical: 'in your head, in your stomach'. Because we experience the terror with Uncle Peter we are unable to criticise him – it is compelling, irresistible, and we have been part of it. The use of the second person allows him to use the present tense, too. If he told it as his personal experience, it would have to be in the past tense and this would reduce the immediacy. It would also personalise it, so that it would become an admission of individual failure. As it is, the passage gives an account of a generalisable, common experience of panic.

Uncle Peter's use of the analogy 'dicky engine' serves several purposes. First, it embeds his role as a pilot in his language. As a consequence, we don't doubt that he was a committed pilot, rather than just a reluctant conscript. Second, it recalls the use of informal terms and contemporary idioms that Mr Hayward makes. This type of language has already accumulated sinister overtones; contrary to the normal expectations this type of language sets up, we know that in *Spies* it indicates something dark. Finally, the word 'dicky' sounds trivial. It makes light of the engine trouble and in doing so conveys the 'stiff upper lip' attitude traditionally adopted by heroes. Embarrassed by shows of emotion, including fear, the upstanding Englishman makes a joke of his troubles – this is so ingrained in Uncle Peter that he makes a passing gesture in that direction even in the midst of his terrible admission of failure.

Embarrassment and humiliation are behind the continuing use of the second person, too. Not only does it make the experience vivid for us and increase our empathy with Uncle Peter, but it helps him to disown the experience. It would be much harder for him to say

CONTEXT

Synesthesia is the experience of mixing sensory perceptions – 'hearing' colours as sounds, for example. Uncle Peter experiencing darkness as a physical feeling in his stomach and his head is a type of synesthesia, yet we are easily able to understand what he means.

that 'I couldn't think, I couldn't move' – and much easier for us to judge him harshly. Embarrassment affects Stephen, too. He is overcome by the horror of having to stand and listen to this account and would rather be anywhere else on Earth when Uncle Peter starts crying. It is like his embarrassment when Mrs Hayward pleaded with him to take the basket and started crying. Stephen is completely unable to deal with displays of emotion, particularly from adults. These outbursts put him in an intolerable situation because they breach the social rules, and Stephen depends heavily on social rules.

PART THREE

CRITICAL APPROACHES

CHARACTERISATION

As in most novels, the **characters** in *Spies* are depicted using several methods. Their own speech and actions, the opinions expressed by others in the **narrative,** and the overt reflections of the **narrator** all play a part in forming our image of the personalities taking part in the action. However, the characters in *Spies* are seen through the eyes of Stephen as a young boy, recollected by Stefan the old man. This means they are **mediated** through him and we have to decide for ourselves how much his feelings colour the way he depicts them. It is a complicated situation. The boy Stephen has an immature assessment of the personalities around him. The older narrator remembers events and conversations as he experienced them in childhood, but with the benefit of maturity he is able to reflect on them and see aspects of the characters' motivation and behaviour that were not apparent to him as a child. Exactly how Frayn is able to convey two, often contradictory, impressions at the same time is examined in more detail in the section **Language: Narrative style.**

STEPHEN/STEFAN

The central **protagonist** is both the boy Stephen and the older narrator Stefan. There is such dislocation between his young and old identities that he could be considered two characters. By returning in maturity to his German birth-name of Stefan, he marks a division between his adult and childhood selves. This is underlined by his unwillingness to recognise or acknowledge aspects of his childhood self. He refers to himself as 'the heir to Stephen's thoughts' (Ch. 7, p. 139), yet he does not seem to be in possession of them. Stefan has less insight into his own earlier motivations and thoughts than is usual for a **first-person narrator.** Indeed, he renounces this role by referring to his younger self in the third person – he often refers to 'Stephen' or 'he'. He struggles to remember or work out what Stephen thought about what happened and even what he did. He even says that he would not recognise

> **CONTEXT**
>
> Frayn has said of Stephen in *Spies*: 'Some stories you need to be inside the heads of the characters and some you don't. With "Spies" you really do need to know what that little boy is thinking about, what he sees, that is the story about how he interprets what's in front of his eyes' (interview with John Tusa, BBC Radio 3, 4 April 2004).

QUESTION

Consider how the older narrator Stefan relates to the young character Stephen. Are they convincingly the same person?

CONTEXT

Frayn's own work as a translator is of literary texts. He has translated, from Russian, Anton Chekhov's plays *Uncle Vanya*, *Three Sisters*, *The Cherry Orchard*, *The Seagull*, *The Sneeze*, *Wild Honey* (Frayn's title; Chekhov left the play without a title) and five one-act plays. He has also translated, from Russian, Leo Tolstoy's comic play *The Fruits of Enlightenment*, Yuri Trifonov's novella *Exchange* and, from French, Jean Anouilh's *Number One*.

himself in photos if it were not for the name on the back (Ch. 2, p. 12). It is more as if he were observing a separate person than remembering his own youth.

STEFAN

The **narrator** is an elderly man. At the end of the novel, we find out what has happened to him in later life. Dissatisfied with a marriage that 'was never quite a real marriage' (Ch. 11, p. 229) he returned to Germany as an adult to try to remake himself. But from a dull job in the engineering department of a polytechnic, he has moved to an equally dull-sounding job writing technical translations of mechanical installation manuals. These jobs are chosen by Frayn to sound uninspiring and unimaginative. A polytechnic does not have the intellectual kudos of a university; everything about his career is unremarkable. His job as a translator suggests that he is attentive to detail, and we do see him making an effort to pin down exactly what happened, to recover as much from his memory as he can to make sense of his story. A translator also needs a very good command of two languages. It makes it an **ironic** choice of career, as the younger Stephen has been so painfully inarticulate and tongue-tied.

A technical translator performs a useful but invisible role, a facilitator rather than a creator. A good translation is one which does not read as though it has been translated at all. Perhaps his contentment with such an unobtrusive role is an extension or consequence of the shyness he shows as a child. He acts, as narrator, as a translator between past and present. But in this role he is far from invisible. We are constantly reminded of his presence as we accompany him on his exploration of the modern-day Close or see him struggle to recall or interpret details of his story.

The very ordinariness of Stefan is important to the scheme of the novel. This is not a tale of how remarkable events produced a remarkable **character**, but a gentler exploration of how incidents may make their mark on an ordinary person.

Stefan is a congenial man. He has a detached, amused view of his earlier self and even of his current life. Perhaps he has been disappointed by what he has made of his life, but he does not

express any overt dissatisfaction with it. The feeling that he might be disappointed comes instead from the way he sums up later events in the last chapter of *Spies*. There is a sense that life has rushed by, that he is rather bewildered as to how it all happened so fast and he reached old age so quickly: 'And now, before I can sort out whether I belong here or there ... my children are grown up, and we have their mother's grave to tend each week' (Ch. 11, p. 230). We can't help but recall his earlier terror of the grave when he says this, but it does not seem to occur to him.

STEPHEN

Stephen is portrayed sympathetically but not sentimentally by his older self. There is much humour in the way that Stefan shows himself as a child, inviting us to laugh gently at him at the same time as engaging with his traumas and inner struggles. He refers to himself as the 'undersized boy with the teapot ears ... open-mouthed and credulous' (Ch. 5, p. 85). His physical appearance led to him being teased by his contemporaries and now even his own older self is teasing him. With the distance given to us by maturity, we are able to see Stephen's troubles with a sense of perspective which is not available to him as a boy.

Stephen's father says to him, 'You've got worse troubles than anyone's ever had before, I know' (Ch. 9, pp. 190–1) and this is how childhood problems seem at the time. Only maturity, and the experience of more and different problems, can change our perspective. But the suffering of the child is as great as that of the adult, even if the particular problem does not warrant the degree of emotional energy that the child invests in it. The mismatch between the suffering and the nature of the problem is a source of both sympathy and humour in *Spies*. This considerate but detached handling of Stephen is characteristic of the narrator's approach.

As a boy, Stephen is constantly held back, dominated and afraid. His fear is the first characteristic we see. In the very first paragraph, the narrator says, 'I'm a child again and everything's before me – all the frightening, half-understood promise of life' (Ch. 1, p. 3). Stephen is checked by Keith's disapproval and by his own fear of looking foolish or acting inappropriately. His strict ideas of social

QUESTION

The Greek philosopher Socrates wrote: 'The unexamined life is not worth living' (*Apologies*, 38a). Investigate Stefan's aims and achievements in examining his life in *Spies*.

CHECK THE BOOK

Literature examining the small episodes that can lead to momentous events in the lives of ordinary people has dominated the novels and drama of the second half of the twentieth century. A key turning point was the publication and production of Arthur Miller's play *Death of a Salesman* (1949) which examines the events leading to the death of an ordinary middle-aged man. It has been hailed as the first American **tragedy**.

CONTEXT

The weedy boy in the Billy Bunter stories published in *Magnet* until 1940 was called 'Skinner Wibley' – not so very different from 'Stephen Wheatley'.

propriety hold him in check; his fear of being teased or bullied limits his actions. He is terrified of looking foolish, of embarrassment: '[W]hich is worse ... To be embarrassed or to be killed?', he asks (Ch. 5, p. 92). He rarely gives full reign to his feelings, and usually only when he is beside himself with terror or grief and is unable to exercise the control that he would like. He shuns demonstrations of emotion and challenging situations that may arouse emotion in him. His natural response to difficulty of any type is to block it out, ignore it or run away from it.

As a young boy, Stephen is painfully shy, aware of what he considers his own social inferiority, and in awe of his domineering friend Keith. Stephen is intensely aware that his family is socially inferior to Keith's family. They have less money, their house is untidy and their possessions less impressive. In many instances, a genuine social or financial distinction is marked in the possessions of Stephen and Keith. But in other cases it is simply Keith's confident assurance of superiority, coupled with Stephen's lack of confidence, that leads Stephen to accept that whatever Keith does or has is right and best. The degree to which Stephen is in awe of Keith and his family is never in doubt: 'The ways of the Haywards were no more open to questioning or comprehension than the domestic arrangements of the Holy Family' (Ch. 2, p. 25). The humour of this line undermines Stephen's adulation. It is a **bathetic** comparison; the level of elevation of the Holy Family is out of all proportion to an assessment of the Haywards. This is an example of how the older **narrator** disowns his earlier views without overt comment.

CONTEXT

Bullying at school was considered part of normal activity in the 1940s. If Stephen had complained to adults he would have been despised for telling tales.

Stephen's acute awareness of his own inferiority makes him unable to imagine that anyone might like him or want to have him around. He refers to Mrs Hayward's 'incomprehensible niceness' (Ch. 3, p. 39) to him, showing how deep his sense of being unworthy goes. It seems that his views are founded in sad experience. He has been teased and bullied in the past, and so is easily dominated by Keith who does not shrink from physical abuse. Stephen is unpopular with the other children, who jeer at him for being small and weedy (a word that has an unfortunate similarity to his name, Wheatley, and so is readily adopted by his tormentors). Stephen has

internalised this criticism and blames himself for being cowardly and weak, intensifying his feeling of inferiority.

Stephen's fear of further criticism and teasing makes him overly compliant. He is easily dominated by Keith. This is partly because he blindly admires Keith, but partly, too, because he dreads censure. The same anxiety is evident in his exchanges with Barbara Berrill in the hideout. The narrator, looking back on his life, says that Keith was 'only the first in a whole series of dominant figures in my life whose disciple I became' (Ch. 2, p. 16). He goes on, tongue in cheek, to say that '[h]is authority was entirely warranted by his intellectual and imaginative superiority' (Ch. 2, p. 16). This clearly is not true: Keith can't spell and his schemes are fanciful but not feasible. He uses his imagination to concoct unbelievable stories about his family's prowess in order to impress Stephen. Stephen, on the other hand, has a powerful imagination that anticipates the consequences of actions or events so vividly that they can terrify him beyond words. He imagines the consequences of events with frightening clarity. He thinks of what will happen after Mrs Hayward is arrested as a spy, down to the detail of Mrs Elmsley having to make lunch for Mr Hayward (Ch. 3, p. 44). He visualises the escape from the house at night by rope, following Mrs Hayward in the darkness (Ch. 3, p. 56), lying in his own coffin (Ch. 9, pp. 192–3), and many more possible scenarios.

Another aspect of this anxious, troubled child is his terror of germs. He is afraid of germs from the slime in the tunnel, from the man at the Barns, from the cigarette that Barbara picks up, and from the blade of the 'bayonet'. Of the children in the Lanes he says, 'Everything about them is plainly laden with germs' (Ch. 6, p. 126). The similarity of the words 'germ' and 'German', and the knowledge that both are undesirable, leads him to assume that there is a link between the two, and so he fears germs from the hidden 'German': 'His Germanness lingers in the air … as insanitary as the germs he's giving off' (Ch. 10, p. 203). Sometimes, Stephen comes across as quite prim and fussy. In the confusion over privet and privy, he says that privies are 'lavatories of some sort, and of some particularly disgusting sort that's full of germs, and that I'm not going to get involved in talking about' (Ch. 5, pp. 97–8).

CONTEXT

In the days before readily available antibiotics, cleanliness was a vitally important way of avoiding infection. The need to avoid 'germs' (bacteria and viruses) would have been instilled into Stephen from a young age.

CHECK THE BOOK
Another novel which examines the results of child abuse during the years of the Second World War is *Goodnight Mr Tom* (1981) by Michelle Magorian. The central character has a classically psychopathic mother who abuses him and kills his baby sister.

and a bully, but at the same time a victim of his father's abuse. He tries to impress Stephen with his exaggerated or invented claims about his family. We cannot know whether his father really killed five Germans in the First World War, but we suspect that he did not. It would be possible for a young man who fought in the First World War to be the father of a boy Keith's age in the Second World War. However, we know that his claim that his parents won the Wimbledon tennis tournament is untrue and we know that the 'bayonet' in the trunk is only a bread knife. Even Stephen doubts that Mr Hayward could have killed Germans with a bayonet attached to a pistol – bayonets are attached to rifles. While this suggests that the whole story is untrue it is not proof.

It takes a while for the extent of Keith's nastiness to become evident. At the start of the novel, it appears only that he is the dominant partner in their friendship, a role bestowed on him by his social superiority and greater confidence. He enjoys appearing superior to Stephen, and Stephen is complicit in this, sometimes deliberately holding back a suggestion or comment in order to let Keith shine. Stephen comments several times on Keith's displeasure when Stephen succeeds or takes the lead, and the displeasure is itself enough to make Stephen hold himself in check the next time. 'I reason slowly, so that Keith can overtake me and resume full control of the operation' (Ch. 5, p. 91). He builds up Keith in his own mind even as he undermines himself: 'Every moment … is a further test of his strength, a further demonstration of his heroism' (Ch. 5, p. 95).

As the novel progresses, we become aware that Keith's home life is not as it seems. There is an extended description of his ordered room, full of valuable and desirable possessions. His playroom, seen through Stephen's eyes, is something of a treasure trove with Keith's toys, unshared with brothers or sisters, 'neatly ranged in drawers and cupboards, often in the boxes they came in' (Ch. 2, p. 17). His room is immaculate, and he spends time oiling his bicycle, looking after his cricket kit and playing with his toys 'all of them in actual working condition' (Ch. 2, p. 18). Only later will we begin to find in this order another sinister indication of the abusive regime under which Keith lives. Everything about the surface of life in his

household is immaculate, but beneath that surface is a very unpleasant reality. Keith is caned by his father for even minor infringements of the family's strict regulations.

Keith is a typical study of a bullied or abused child. He relishes exercising power over Stephen, taking out on Stephen the feelings of powerlessness and resentment that his father instils in him. It is common for abused and bullied children to mete out the same treatment to their friends or, later, their own children. At the start of the novel, Keith is already displaying some of his father's mannerisms, showing his disapproval of Stephen with a particular facial expression – a dropping of the eyelids, or a thin smile 'as sharp as the edge of a sharpened blade' (Ch. 5, p. 98). Later, Keith adopts his father's chilling use of familiarity and endearments, calling him 'old bean', when he is intimidating or threatening Stephen. Finally, he copies his father's knife torment, holding the point of the bread knife to Stephen's throat while trying to coax information from him when he does not get what he wants from Stephen. That Mr Hayward does the same to his wife is clear from her use of a cravat tied high on her neck even on the hottest days of summer. It is only after Stephen has suffered the same fate at the hands of Keith that he recognises the reason for the cravat, but it has already been mentioned on two separate occasions.

Keith is neither bright nor popular. Stephen decides not to mention his misspelling of 'private', but is aware of Keith's inferiority in this regard. Mrs Hayward, on seeing the sign, is not surprised that Keith could not spell the word properly indicating that it is not just a momentary lapse. Barbara says that the other children don't like Keith: 'He's so stuck-up. Everyone except you really hates him' (Ch. 5, p. 99). This seems to be true, as he is never part of the crowd of children in the street who follow the policeman or play together. He is at a private preparatory school and not the local school attended by the other children. After the end of the main action of the novel, he will be further removed still, being sent away to boarding school.

Keith uses Stephen to boost his own confidence and impression of himself. He manipulates Stephen into looking foolish, forcing

> **CONTEXT**
>
> In the English public school system, children attend a preparatory school between the ages of seven and thirteen. After taking the Common Entrance exam, a boy then moves on to day or boarding school. In the English state school system, children in the 1940s took an exam called the 11 Plus at the age of eleven. On the basis of the outcome they went either to a grammar (higher tier) school or a secondary modern (the lower tier).

Stephen to try to guess what he is thinking or to anticipate the next stage in a plan and then mocking him if he cannot. Such is his hold over Stephen that sometimes he can belittle Stephen with a practised look of disapproval. Stephen goes along with this, recognising and responding to the signs that he is supposed to feel crushed. At other times Keith is more direct in his disapproval or mockery. When he deduces that Stephen did not look at the man by the embankment because he was afraid, he accuses him of acting like 'a little baby' (Ch. 6, p. 124). He cannot be impressed by anything Stephen achieves because to do so robs him of the chance to demonstrate his own superiority. He also needs Stephen in order to be able to shine himself. Stephen is aware of this: 'Without me there's no one for him to be braver than' (Ch. 6, p. 125). Stephen is amazed that he is invariably welcome at Keith's house. He supposes that his social inferiority should exclude him. But Mrs Hayward is aware that Keith has no friends, and is glad that someone takes an interest in him. She does not seem to know her son well, though, because she accuses Stephen of leading Keith astray and giving him ridiculous ideas that will get him into trouble. Even Stephen is astonished at this.

MRS HAYWARD

A more unlikely German spy than Mrs Hayward is hard to imagine. At the start of the book, she comes across as a leisured, elegant and serene woman entirely typical of her social class and era. Everything about her and her house is perfect, ordered, neat and beautiful. Even her chickens 'lived irreproachably elegant lives, parading haughtily about a spacious kingdom' (Ch. 2, p. 20) and laying clean eggs. Stephen sees Mrs Hayward as a paragon of 'grace and serenity' (Ch. 2, p. 26). She appears even-tempered and cheerful. She does little all day – Stephen says she rests in her room or on the sofa with a library book – and has a cleaning lady to look after the house.

Although Stephen misjudges the reason for it, he recognises an air of falsity in Mrs Hayward's jollity. He and Keith take the artificiality of her manner as evidence that she is in fact a spy. On a first reading, and at this stage of the novel, we might assume that any stiltedness is only the mannered behaviour common in a woman of her social class during the 1940s. Later, we realise that her

home life is oppressive and violent and that the veneer of respectability which Stephen mistakes for a false identity conceals a different type of sinister hidden life.

Her perfect exterior disguises, we presume, fear and misery as she lives under the tyranny of Mr Hayward's rule. She maintains an appearance of calm even under extreme duress, demonstrating immense self-control. When she discovers her husband holding the basket that she had given Stephen to take to the Barns, she betrays no hint of panic: '"Oh, thank you," she says calmly … "Aren't those the things you and Keith borrowed for your camp?"' (Ch. 9, p. 189). We never discover the full extent of the punishment she may have suffered as a result of this incident with the basket, but she is wearing a cravat next time Stephen sees her – evidence, he later surmises, of an injured throat. She must have known the likely consequences of Mr Hayward's discovery, yet she calmly sends Stephen to find Keith, betraying no fear or other emotion. She is brave and resolute. After the episode with the thermos flask, she is soon slipping away from her vigilant husband to deliver a message for Stephen to carry to the Barns. Feigning a broken shoe, she returns towards the house to look for him in the hideout.

We never discover for certain to what extent she has taken Uncle Peter to her bosom, in Stephen's phrase. Whether they are having an affair, whether it is consummated or whether it is unrequited passion on Uncle Peter's part is never clarified. The 'x' in the cigarette packet suggests his love is reciprocated, but the inability to pin down the meaning of 'x' is developed at such length in the novel that we cannot be certain. She remains a closed a book. To Stephen's eyes, any demonstration of emotion on her part is embarrassing and a violation of his image of her perfect serenity. If there were any signal, we feel he would have obstinately ignored it.

However, it is not just Mrs Hayward's elegance that leads Stephen to be embarrassed by her having to sit in the dirt to talk to him, and having to reveal her distress and need when she asks him to take the basket. His feelings about her are confused. He sees her, as an adult and the mother of a friend, as almost a different species, her motivation and feelings intractable to the normal reasoning he could

> **CONTEXT**
>
> A 1942 book of sewing patterns for women's fashions describes the cravat as follows: 'The modern adaptation of the cravat is about 21 inches long and 9 inches wide with slight shaping in the centre. It is tied in a simple overhand knot with ends spread.'

apply to another child. It is when her actions seem to cross this invisible boundary between adulthood and childhood that Stephen cannot cope. His inclination to turn away, to say nothing and wait for the exchanges to end, makes it difficult for us to garner information about Mrs Hayward – she is kept at arm's length by his refusal to engage with her. Her diary reveals nothing except the day-to-day routine of her life, her menstrual cycle and (we presume) the infrequent sexual activity with her husband indicated by the occasional exclamation marks. She is careful – the cigarette packet contains no evidence, only the 'x' to indicate any bond and nothing to reveal her identity.

MR HAYWARD

Like Mrs Hayward, Mr Hayward seems to have no daytime occupation. He spends his time in his garage or garden, whistling and intimidating people. This gives him the opportunity to keep a careful eye on his wife. At the start of the novel, Stephen sees the garage as a 'wonderful private kingdom' (Ch. 2, p. 21). He is in awe of Mr Hayward's tools and manly activity in the garage, and in particular of his gleaming (if useless) car. Yet the control he exercises over his neat home and garden mirrors the control he exercises over his family. He is a bully who abuses his son and his wife. The neatly ordered exterior that is presented to society hides a world of abusive behaviour and cruelty. He canes Keith for even slight infractions of his rules, and by the end of the novel he is apparently injuring his wife as well as watching her every move. When it looks as though they are taking a companionable stroll down the street together, Mr Hayward is actually making sure his wife cannot escape from his sight.

His cruel behaviour is particularly chilling because it is preceded by a display of false geniality. He signals his displeasure with a thin smile and by addressing his victim (usually Keith) familiarly as 'old bean' or 'chap'. Keith is learning to follow his father's example, as the victims of bullies so often do. Mr Hayward is particularly inarticulate, often speaking in clipped, abbreviated phrases that do not form themselves into sentences: 'Silly games. Don't play them' (Ch. 9, p. 187). However, conjecture about any link between his mode of speech and his cruelty is not encouraged by the novel.

CONTEXT

Mr Hayward's ownership of a car sets him apart on the Close. The first Highway Code and Road Traffic Act was passed in 1931, eight years before the start of the war. Mr Hayward must have had his car since before 1939, when car factories were forced to make machinery for the war effort.

We can be certain of little of Mr Hayward's background because we have only Keith's account of his past to go on. Keith is an unreliable witness. He tries to aggrandise himself by boasting about his parents and their achievements. He says that Mr Hayward fought in the First World War and killed five Germans. Mr Hayward is now in the Home Guard, so is presumably too old to be enlisted. Keith says that the Home Guard is a cover for Secret Service activity, but we have no reason to believe this is true. Is Mr Hayward a bully because he is a coward, or because he was traumatised in the First World War? Did he invent the tale about the heroic killing of Germans because he is ashamed at not having fought, or did Keith invent it? Or is it true to some degree? These questions are not answered by the novel.

BARBARA BERRILL

Barbara is a minor **character**, but important as the only other child with whom Stephen engages on a roughly equal footing. She is talkative and somewhat bossy, but not as domineering as Keith. She can be manipulative, goading Stephen by trying to show that he is immature or ignorant, but she can also be genuinely friendly. She taunts him with her superior knowledge of what adults get up to, jeering when he reveals gaps in his knowledge. She is sometimes spiteful, but relents and is kinder again when Stephen makes it clear that he is hurt by her remarks. Her behaviour falls within the normal range of childish competitiveness and teasing – it does not amount to the unpleasantness that Keith engages in.

She is open and honest about the limitations in her own knowledge. She is confident enough to admit that she has not smoked, and to ask Stephen how to do it. She shares information about her friendships and asks Stephen to be her friend. Her father is away fighting in the war and her mother apparently has a boyfriend, a fact which Barbara accepts without question and without apparent thought. She and her household come to represent to Stephen a chaotic, relaxed and appealing wildness full of promise. Stephen has earlier repeated the gossip, 'everyone says they're running wild' (Ch. 2, p. 13), and even Barbara herself speaks of her mother complaining that their father is not there to keep them in order. She is the counterpoint to Keith, who represents control, order and

> **CONTEXT**
>
> Child abuse has been differently defined since the later years of the twentieth century and it is unlikely that Mr Hayward's treatment of Keith would have been considered particularly unusual. Corporal punishment was used in schools as well as homes. Even so, Mr Hayward goes beyond the bounds of acceptable behaviour as he evidently injures his wife with a knife in the same way that Keith later injures Stephen.

> **CONTEXT**
>
> Barbara Berrill's surname may recall the name of 'Beryl the Peril', a mischievous character in the Denis the Menace strip cartoon published in *The Topper* comic from 1953.

suffocating formality. Although Stephen begins by not wanting anything to do with her, he softens. When he revisits the Close as an old man, he imagines for a moment that an elderly woman at Number 6 is Barbara. Perhaps it is – we never find out – but it suggests that he harbours some residual affection for her. There is more about Barbara's character in **Extended commentaries – Text 1.**

STEPHEN'S FAMILY

There is no overlap between Stephen's family in the past and Stefan's family in the present of the novel. Stephen's mother, father and brother, Geoff, feature in the **narrative** set during the Second World War, but all are dead by the time the older Stefan is recalling events. In their place, his family consists of his own son, daughter and grandchildren, none of whom is named in the book. He has also been married twice; his second wife is dead. Although none of the **characters** is the same, Stefan's son resembles Geoff in the only spoken words he has. When Stefan's daughter asks if they will have a contact address for him in England, it is his son who responds: '"Memory Lane, perhaps," suggests my son drily' (Ch. 1, p. 6). The sardonic tone is characteristic of Geoff in earlier times.

The most important member of Stephen's family for the novel is his father. In a counterpoint to Keith's father, Mr Wheatley is kind and mild-mannered. While Mr Hayward is 'like an ogre in his cave' (Ch. 7, p. 144), Mr Wheatley is 'like some mild-natured furry animal' (Ch. 2, p. 26). He is quietly affectionate, worrying about the bullying that Stephen is subjected to, and putting his arms around Stephen after Keith has injured his throat. His response to Stephen's injury is gentle. While Mrs Wheatley 'grabs', 'marches' and 'demands', Mr Wheatley 'gently undoes [his] collar and examines [his] throat' and washes the wound with 'tenderness' (Ch. 10, p. 213). When he shouts at Stephen after finding him outside in the night, it is the most agitated that Stephen has ever seen him (Ch. 6, p. 119).

Mr Wheatley seems dull to Stephen: 'The presence of Stephen's father was scarcely noticeable. He was out at an office somewhere all day and often all evening, doing a job, too dull to describe'

(Ch. 2, p. 26). Indeed, Stephen is not curious about this as the working world of adults holds no interest for him: 'Vanishing and reappearing seemed a full enough job description for all practical purposes' (Ch. 7, pp. 139–40). Yet he is solid and reliable. The occasional glimpses of how his earlier life as a Jew in Nazi Germany may have affected him probably go unnoticed on a first reading when we are not aware of his background: '"I don't like bullying," he says, "I've seen too much of it in my lifetime"' (Ch. 10, p. 213). Untold (and unquestioned) volumes of earlier suffering may be hidden in this mild remark. The insistence that Stephen stay in on Friday evenings, which irks Stephen, is a Jewish tradition his son later adopts himself. That Stephen thinks his father dreary is a tribute to his skill at being unobtrusive as both a father and an intelligence worker. Spies must go unnoticed if they are to be successful, as Stephen himself recognises. To pass without comment is essential to Mr Wheatley's war work for the British and his involvement with German refugees. It is ironic that Stephen, even when older, never shows any interest in finding out about his father's secret activities. Perhaps in contrast to the trouble they would have experienced in Germany, Mr Wheatley is content to give Stephen an ordinary childhood. He succeeds; looking back, the narrator says Stephen 'must have loved his family, because loving your family was the ordinary arrangement in life, and everything in Stephen's family ... was quite extraordinarily ordinary' (Ch. 2, p. 28).

Little is revealed about Stephen's mother. She is rather a caricature – rushed, impatient with Stephen getting his clothes dirty or spending too much time at Keith's house where he might be in the way, and fussing over his school clothes, messy room or dirty shoes. She defers to Stephen's father, leaving him to deal with anything difficult, such as bullying and teasing, and explaining the meaning of 'sheeny' (Ch. 4, p. 64). It seems to Stephen, in words that conjure up all the harshness of a child who takes his parents' love for granted, that 'There's something so hopelessly ordinary about her that it's difficult to take account of her existence' (Ch. 3, p. 42), and indeed the book barely does take account of her existence. Together, the couple and Geoff form an 'unsatisfactory family' (Ch. 4, p. 65) as far as Stephen is concerned and, misguidedly, 'where he longed to be was at Keith's house' (Ch. 2, p. 28).

> **CONTEXT**
>
> When Stephen says that his father's father and two brothers 'had all been taken and murdered' (Ch. 11, p. 229) he may mean that they were taken to a concentration camp where they were later killed, or that they were dragged from their houses and shot or beaten to death – the fate of many Jews under Nazi rule.

UNCLE PETER

For the greater part of *Spies*, Uncle Peter is an 'absent presence' as
the RAF pilot who is supposedly flying bombing missions over
Germany. But at the same time he is present, though unrecognised,
as the man at the Barns. Just as Stephen is also Stefan and the two
are very different, Uncle Peter is also the very different man at the
Barns.

Uncle Peter is idealised and idolised. The picture that Stephen paints
of him returning to the Close, surrounded by adoring children, is of
an archetypal war hero recalling propaganda materials from both
the First and Second World Wars. Since he is wearing his RAF
uniform in his wedding photograph, he may be a career pilot rather
than a conscript. It is impossible to tell, since his daughter Milly
may be young enough to have been conceived after the start of the
war. However, his bookshelves contain old adventure stories which
Keith is sometimes allowed to borrow (Ch. 2, p. 25), suggesting that
he has enjoyed romantic notions of being an action hero. Uncle
Peter's iconic status reflects on Auntie Dee, and even the untidiness
of their house 'glowed with a kind of sacred light, like a saint and
his attributes in a religious painting' (Ch. 2, pp. 24–5). (There is
more about religious **imagery** in **Language: Narrative style**.)

The man in the Barns, on the other hand, is a desperate, sick, broken
individual. A fugitive or refugee, he has no status in society and lives
beyond the edges of civilisation, even beyond the Cottages which
are inhabited by the lowliest people in the local society. He is
dependent on Mrs Hayward and Auntie Dee for food, clothes and
medicine. If he tried to rejoin society, he would be court-martialled
for desertion. When he comes near the Close, the police are called.
He is mistaken for a tramp, a peeping Tom and, by Stephen and
Keith, for a German. Stephen remarks with delight that the
supposed tramp is '*that* low in the table of human precedence' that
he's 'scared of *me*' (Ch. 6, p. 130). This figure is as far from a war
hero as he could be.

When the man at the Barns finally speaks to Stephen and we get to
hear his own story, the polar opposites of the tramp (or German)
and Uncle Peter the hero collide. There is more to this than the

CONTEXT

Conscription
swelled the ranks
of the RAF during
the Second World
War, but men had
to volunteer to be
trained as pilots –
no one was forced
to learn to fly.

CONTEXT

Desertion during a
war is a serious
crime, and Uncle
Peter could have
expected to be
court-martialled
and punished if
discovered. During
the First and
Second World
Wars, there was
little tolerance of
or sympathy for
combatants who
fell victim to stress
or other
psychological
problems.

unpicking of **icons** in the novel. We are forced to see how wrong ideas about other people may be. This paves the way for Stefan's revelations about his own identity, too, and recalls how the public faces of Mr and Mrs Hayward are very different from the private realities.

The man at the Barns and Uncle Peter both are and are not the same person. It is impossible for Stephen to accommodate such vastly different ideas about him. Although his older self wonders whether he really failed to recognise Uncle Peter, it is more that he refused to recognise him. Later, when he sees Milly's pushchair outside Keith's house, he hears the voice of the man at the Barns whispering his name: 'I close my mind to the memory', he says (Ch. 10, p. 207), denying the equivalence of Uncle Peter and the man.

Yet in the collision of these two archetypes a real human character emerges – Peter Tracey. When the man at the Barns becomes the pilot, the trauma he describes is all too real and human; it is something that we can **identify** and sympathise with. His experience of terror, of losing his nerve, is instantly recognisable. He is distinguished as an individual by his professed love for 'Bobs' (Mrs Hayward) and the terrible admission that he already knew that he loved her when he married her sister. Peter still has a hint of the pilot's bravura about him. He uses understatement when describing his plight; he says that it 'gets a bit bleak, lying here' (Ch. 10, p. 201) and likens himself to a 'dicky engine' (Ch. 10, p. 203). But his despair comes through increasingly as he relaxes into talking. He reveals that he listens to the trains, imagining himself speeding away from the Barns on every one of them. He is unable to bring himself to name his wife, calling her 'Milly's mother' (Ch. 10, p. 202). His desperate wish to leave something for Bobs is painful to read. He cannot write anything that will be meaningful, and fixes on his silk map as the only token he can give. That and the single phrase 'For ever' (Ch. 10, p. 205) – both of which Stephen fails to deliver.

We cannot be sure how Peter Tracey dies, whether by accident or suicide, but death is clearly the only end possible for him. He could be a tragic hero, if given sufficient development of his own. As it is, his passing goes undiscussed. Auntie Dee moves away and Mrs

CONTEXT

By the end of the Second World War, the RAF numbered 1,208,000 men and women, of whom 185,000 were air crew. 70,000 members of the RAF were killed during the course of the war.

Hayward reveals nothing but disappears back into her abusive marriage. All trace of Peter is expunged, from everywhere except Stephen's memory and even there he has been denied and locked away for nearly sixty years.

AUNTIE DEE

Auntie Dee is never a real presence in the novel, and has little development as a **character**; she has no directly observed interactions with Stephen. She is the essence of 'auntness' in Stephen's view, and as such it is right that she is warm, bustling, talkative, fussy – and an embarrassment to Keith. She and her lively, bubbly toddler, Milly, are the counterpoint to the strict and tidy family of her sister, Mrs Hayward. She is presumably unaware of any relationship her sister and her husband may be having, or of her husband's infatuation if the couple are not actually having an affair. At the end of the novel, the **narrator** tells us that the sisters fell out and Auntie Dee moved away after Uncle Peter was posted as missing, so perhaps the implication is that she discovered their relationship then.

Auntie Dee has a largely functional role in the novel. She provides an excuse for Mrs Hayward to go up the road all the time. She is involved with Mrs Hayward in sending supplies to Peter at the Barns. She basks in the war hero's reflected glory and is a reminder of it while he is away. She apparently still loves her husband as she has, according to gossip, been seen kissing him. For Stephen, she seems to represent a middle path between his own unsatisfactory household and the socially elevated Hayward household. At Auntie Dee's the atmosphere is relaxed, there is a normal level of untidiness and yet treats are still abundant.

The photograph of Auntie Dee and Mrs Hayward as children prompts Stephen's stunning realisation that the women are still sisters. It stands as an emblem of the incomprehensible transition from child to adult. That they are pretending to be child and adult in the photo adds an extra dimension, and perhaps illuminates Auntie Dee's relationship with her sister now. Mrs Hayward is the elder sister, and perhaps still retains some level of authority over Auntie Dee.

 CHECK THE NET

If Mrs Hayward is in her thirties during the 1940s, she would have been about Keith's age in the 1920s. For an indication of how she and Auntie Dee may have dressed in the photograph, see **www.fashion-era.com** and follow links to the 1920s.

THEMES

WAR

The Second World War (1939–45) forms the backdrop to *Spies*. It provides the framework in which the action takes place, but has little impact on the day-to-day activity of Stephen and Keith until they decide that Mrs Hayward is a German spy. Even then, it is as a remote idea that the war shapes their actions. Stephen drops references to the propaganda of the day – the Duration, the War Effort, the blackout – and there are small details of daily life that are constant reminders that it is wartime, but there is no trauma or worry associated with these. It is very dark at night, because the blackout means there can be no lights showing. Food scraps are collected in buckets for the pigs. Building in the area has stopped until after the war, the land cleared for building has become overgrown again, and one area they play in is the ruins of a bombed house. Later, Stefan recalls the vapour trails across the sky, the searchlights and the flares (Ch. 2, p. 10) but these are not mentioned in the recalled action; presumably the Blitz had taken place before the events of the novel. Neither Stephen nor Keith has a parent serving in the armed forces, although Keith's father is in the Home Guard and attends weekly drill.

For Keith and Stephen, the war is a source of excitement, potential heroism and adventure. Keith creates an image of his father as a great hero of the First World War, killing German soldiers at close range with a bayonet. He exaggerates his father's involvement in the Home Guard as being part of the Secret Service. It is something else to be included in their games and to give their lives colour. Although they play in the ruins of Miss Durrant's bombed house, they do not really think about the war and what it means. They do not see it as a threat or as frightening. In all Stephen's panics about disasters that may befall him, being bombed by Germans never features. His dislike of Germans is something that has been instilled in him by war propaganda and by his schoolmates, and is unquestioning and uninformed. He assumes that Germans have some link with germs. Germans are beyond Stephen's knowledge and understanding and he is not held accountable for his hostility

CONTEXT

Frayn also grew up in the Second World War. He told interviewer Marcy Kahan: 'We all grew up during the war, but it didn't affect us as much because we were children at the time.'

CHECK THE NET

Use a search engine to look for Second World War propaganda posters. There are several sources of these online.

towards them – it has been imposed upon him and is part of the fabric of his childhood, like the war.

For some of the lesser characters, the war has a more immediate and real impact. Barbara Berrill's father is away fighting, and her mother has apparently taken a lover in his absence. Auntie Dee's husband (Uncle Peter) is a pilot in the Air Force and is thought to be on a tour of duty. Every time a policeman comes down the street, the fear that Uncle Peter has been shot down is uppermost in everyone's minds. But this is a grown-up concern and does not bother Stephen.

The image of the war for most of the novel is defined by the exhilaration of Stephen and Keith at the prospect of uncovering Mrs Hayward as a German spy. It is a source of excitement and potential intrigue, fun for young boys. Uncle Peter is seen as a great war hero, whose glory rubs off on those associated with him. His photograph on the mantelpiece is an **icon** of war heroism, and gives Auntie Dee a 'saint-like' glow (Ch. 2, p. 24). When he once visited the Close in his uniform, children crowded around him to admire and touch his insignia. It is an idealistic picture, reminiscent of the propaganda posters of the day, and of the many films that glorified the war in the years just after it ended.

This sanitised and glorifying image of the war is overturned by later events in the novel. Reality – in war as in everything else – is shown to be a lot more complicated, messy and unpleasant than the boys' view allows. Instead of a brave war hero, Uncle Peter is a broken man – sick and lost and hiding in a hole underground. The reality of air battles is not of dashing pilots and brave manoeuvres, but of terrified young men who may lose their nerve, as Uncle Peter has done, and who then put at risk the lives of their colleagues as well as themselves. There is a glimpse of a crashed plane, taken away on a train at the end of the novel, which serves as a reminder of the fate that Uncle Peter feared. The whole edifice of war as adventure which Stephen and Keith have constructed and inhabited is brought crashing down by Uncle Peter's brief, terrible **narrative**. For him, too, war had originally looked like a game he could play and win: 'You start playing some game, and you're the brave one, you're the

great hero. But the game goes on and on, and it gets more and more frightening' (Ch. 10, p. 203). In recounting what happened to him, he uses the second person, distancing the awful memories and the shame they instil by refusing to acknowledge them as his own experience. His refusal to use the first person has another effect, too. While removing it from his own experience, he makes it ours. He tells us what to feel, how to imagine it to make it vivid and real: 'You can't think, you can't move. You can't see, you can't hear. Everything's drowned by this great scream of terror in the darkness … and it's coming out of *you*' (Ch. 10, p. 203). This makes the experience potentially universal, accessible to each of us. Uncle Peter is not unusual in being unable to bear the pressure of flying bombing raids; it is a response that anyone and everyone may have.

Frayn allows no national monopoly on the sufferings of war. The agonies of Stefan's aunt are equally vividly imagined as 'the unbreathable gases from the burning house filled their dark cellar ten thousand feet below him, or someone like him' (Ch. 11, p. 234). First we have sympathy for Uncle Peter's plight, and then for that of his victims – we are not allowed to forget the purpose of his flying his plane. There is no moral censure: the pilot and the bombed mother are equally worthy of our sympathy and in some way equally guiltless. Stefan, whose family was largely annihilated by the war, seems to have no hard feelings towards either side, only regret. There is no comment on the political situation that created the war – this would not be appropriate as the action is shown from Stephen's point of view and the focus of the novel is on the impact on individuals. The novel shows the war as something that happened to ordinary people, to the helpless Miss Durrant and Stefan's aunt, killed at home, and to the conscripted men on both sides who, like Uncle Peter, were forced to fly the bombers.

CHILDHOOD AND MATURITY

A central theme of *Spies* is the gulf between adulthood and childhood that is difficult, if not impossible, to bridge. Looking back, the adult finds it hard to imagine what it was like to be a child. **Ironically**, to demonstrate this great gulf between the mature and

QUESTION

In Chapters 9 and 10 there are parallels between Mrs Hayward and Uncle Peter which serve to draw them together, even though they never meet in front of us. Peter's words recall her saying to Stephen 'Life can be so cruel sometimes. It all seems so easy for a start' (Ch. 9, p. 180). How obvious does this connection appear on a first reading of the novel?

CHECK THE BOOK

Max Arthur's *Forgotten Voices of the Second World War: A New History of World War Two in the Words of the Men and Women Who Were There* (Ebury Press, 2004) is a compilation of records from the Imperial War Museum sound archive of interviews with people who lived through and served in the Second World War.

immature self, Frayn is accomplishing exactly what Stefan claims is impossible – he is recalling and recreating how it feels to be a child. He captures the naivety of childhood, and the strange mix of knowingness and ignorance that characterised children of the Second World War period in England. Stephen knows Latin, complex maths, the exports of Canada – but is unable to imagine that his teenage brother might kiss a girl, or that a woman whose husband is away for a long time might take a lover. He accepts Keith's tales of a wild ape-man, a serial murderer and that they can build a railway and communications system all with unquestioning boyhood enthusiasm. Yet there is a lot about the child's state of mind that is lost to the adult. The **narrator** asks **rhetorical questions** again and again about how much the child knew, whether he noticed the inconsistencies and anomalies in the stories he was accepting and taking part in.

For Stephen, adults may as well be a different species. He finds it inconceivable, as children do, that the adults surrounding him were once children with the same worries and preoccupations as he has. He finds it impossible to imagine Auntie Dee and Mrs Hayward as sisters. The idea that sisters stay sisters when they grow up is almost incomprehensible to him. On the other side of the gulf, Stefan barely recognises himself (Ch. 2, p. 12), and struggles to remember what he thought or felt.

Between childhood and adulthood is adolescence and the process of growing up. While Stephen is just beginning to enter this middle ground his brother, Geoff, is the token fully fledged adolescent in the book. He is preoccupied with girls and smoking, speaks his mind plainly, and adopts verbal mannerisms that annoy Stephen. He is understood by both adults and children, yet ignored by both, too. More often than not, he is told to be quiet.

Stephen is beginning to undergo the process of changing into an adult himself. Even though the action of the novel takes place over only a few weeks, noticeable changes take place in him. From finding that Barbara makes him squirm at her unpleasant girliness, he finds himself entranced by the hairs on her skin (Ch. 5, p. 99) and even the bobbly purse that he initially despised. Yet, he is not

CONTEXT

Michael Frayn has said 'one's feelings about oneself shift and change all the time ... and one is to some extent a stranger to oneself' (interview with John Tusa, BBC Radio 3, 4 April 2004).

CONTEXT

Geoff later dies of lung cancer (Ch. 11, p. 232). The dangers of cigarette smoking were not known in the 1940s.

exactly bowled over by their tentative sexual experiment: he 'manage[s] not to flinch' and politely says that the kiss is 'Quite nice' (Ch. 9, p. 186). With the cigarette he shares with Barbara, Stephen imagines he starts to approach adulthood: 'I have a sense of freedom, as if I'm no longer bound by the rules and restrictions of childhood ... I'm on the verge of understanding mysteries that have been closed to me' (Ch. 8, pp. 166–7).

It is not all plain sailing. Stephen moves backwards and forwards, sometimes being more childish and at other times more grown up. He can still crawl into his parents' bed when night terrors beset him. And his rosy view of adulthood is soon corrected: 'I'm leaving behind the old tunnels and terrors of childhood – and stepping into a new world of even darker tunnels and more elusive terrors' (Ch. 9, p. 180).

MEMORY

The narration of *Spies* is prompted by an unsolicited memory; it becomes an exercise in reconstructing the events around the memory. The smell of privet is the trigger which leads Stefan to revisit the scene of his childhood to work out why the scent is so evocative for him.

Sense memories are vivid throughout the novel, and even when Stefan has difficulty recalling events he is often very precise about how things felt, looked, smelled or sounded. Although he can't recall exactly what happened, he says, 'I can feel in my fingertips, as clearly as the scaliness of the snake [buckle], the hopeless bagginess of the failed garter beneath the turned-down top' of his sock (Ch. 2, p. 13). He vividly recreates the delights of tea at Keith's house: 'I taste the chocolate spread on the thick plank of bread. I feel in my fingertips the diamond pattern incised in the tumblers of lemon barley' (Ch. 2, p. 28). There are many vivid details like this that help to recreate the scene so that we can feel it as keenly as Stephen did. These recalled details cover all five senses – sight, sound, taste, smell and touch – and relate to interior feelings as well as those coming from external stimuli. In the hideout, his 'knees ache from crouching. I try to shift my weight from one leg to the other' (Ch. 4, p. 78). In Mr Hayward's garage, '[t]he air's

> **CONTEXT**
>
> Chocolate and hazelnut spread was invented in Italy in the 1940s when chocolate was in short supply because of the war. The aim was to make chocolate go further by combining it with other ingredients. It was first made in blocks to be sliced; it was later made into a spread sold in jars. The first purely chocolate spread (without nuts) was Choba, invented in the Netherlands in 1948. It is unlikely that Stephen could, in fact, have had chocolate spread in England in the early 1940s. As Italy was at war with England, Italian confectionery would not have been available to him.

CONTEXT

At the start of Frayn's novel *Headlong*, the narrator explains how he will go about recreating the events of his story from memory: 'I shall have to go back in time to the very beginning, and relive what happened as it happened, from one moment to the next, explaining exactly what I thought as I thought it ... without the distortions of hindsight' (*Headlong*, Faber & Faber, 1999, p. 2). In trying to present everything as Stephen experienced it, Frayn again tries to avoid the 'distortions of hindsight' in *Spies*.

full of the smell of sawdust and oil, of concrete and car, and of fear' (Ch. 9, p. 187).

Sometimes, Stephen pieces together memories as though they are parts of a jigsaw puzzle, acting like a detective in uncovering clues as to what happened or when. He pins down the events to early summer because of the apple blossom. He realises that the covered jug of lemonade must have been outside because it was the wind that made the beads chink against the jug. This creates the impression that there is a definite reality that, in an ideal situation, can be uncovered by careful analysis of memories and the evidence they present. It is not an ideal situation, though, and he stumbles over things he has forgotten or did not observe at the time. What the **narrator** gives us is not history as it happened, but history as he can best reconstruct it from a combination of incomplete memories and logical reasoning.

What Stefan struggles to remember most of all is what he thought, what he knew and what he understood as a child. He repeatedly poses **rhetorical questions** to tackle this, asking what he knew, what he understood, and whether he saw any contradiction in the things he seemed to believe. He tries to work out what he must have felt or thought from the evidence of his actions, but here his method falls down rather. It can tell him what happened but not why something happened, what motivated people to act as they did. The actions he remembers don't reveal anything very certain about his motivations or inner state and even less of those of other people.

The fact that the narrator so frequently highlights his difficulty in recalling accurate memories, and returns again and again to the **conceit** of the novel as a series of remembered and reconstructed events, forces us to confront the real truth, that Frayn has invented a narrator who struggles to remember and understand the plot of his own story. Surely we must ask why he has done this. It must be to persuade us to think about the very nature of remembered reality. Is something real as it happened, or is it real as it is remembered? Since different people recall the same event in different ways, is there any objective reality at all?

IMAGINATION

Imagination is a driving force in the action of *Spies* and is closely tied to memory. The original premise, that Mrs Hayward is a spy, is acknowledged by Stephen as an imaginative construct which the two boys choose to act upon as just the latest in a string of adventures: 'Keith's words came out of nowhere ... they were spontaneously created in the moment they were uttered ... they were a blind leap of pure fantasy' (Ch. 2, p. 33). He does accept that the words could show intuition, too – that perhaps Keith had picked up on something secretive in his mother's manner. But the idea that Mrs Hayward is a spy was effectively an invention around which another adventure could be constructed. The game of watching and spying on Mrs Hayward would have been harmless enough – only intrusive and annoying – if it were not for the unfortunate coincidence that she really did have something to hide.

Both Keith and Stephen have active imaginations, but they are active in different ways. Keith comes up with schemes and explanations that make him look clever. Stephen's imagination foresees the possible consequences of actions, what might have happened in other circumstances. Often, these imagined realities are terrifying for Stephen. The most frightening is his vision of himself in his coffin (Ch. 9, p. 192), but the narrative is full of tiny imagined scenarios. In his mind's eye, he sees Uncle Peter's death: 'the live rail leapt out at him, and the passing trains cut him in pieces' (Ch. 10, p. 221). He imagines a German airman collapsing with his parachute to the ground after being shot down (Ch. 8, p. 170); he supposes this is the man at the Barns: 'I see the whole story' (Ch. 8, p. 169). His imagination conjures up all kinds of mini-narratives that take the story in different directions until it is recalled to its 'true' line. So he imagines Uncle Peter coming home to find Auntie Dee has been arrested as a spy (Ch. 4, p. 70), and he imagines seeing Mrs Hayward sending Morse code messages (Ch. 4, p. 61). Sometimes, these deviations in the **narrative** are presented in the same voice as the 'real' narrative and without any immediate indication that they are imaginings until after we have been carried along by them for a moment: '"She's a German spy," I explain. No, I don't say the words. Do I?' (Ch. 5, p. 100).

> **CONTEXT**
>
> Frayn has said of the **character** Werner Heisenberg at the heart of his play *Copenhagen*: 'Heisenberg, [it] seems to me, didn't have absolute access to his intentions and none of us does' (interview with John Tusa, BBC Radio 3, 4 April 2004).

> **CONTEXT**
>
> Michael Frayn had a similar friend himself, who provided the imaginative input into their games: 'I had no imagination ... All the imagination was provided by this great friend of mine on whom the Keith character in my novel is based. He had a very lively imagination. He thought of the games we played' (interview with John Tusa, BBC Radio 3, 4 April 2004).

CONTEXT

Some modern
theoretical
physicists
postulate a series
of infinite parallel
universes in which
different realities
coexist. This would
allow a universe in
which Mrs
Hayward is a
German spy and
one in which she is
not. In *The Fabric
of Reality: The
Science of Parallel
Universes and Its
Implications*
(1998), David
Deustch suggests
that these parallel
universes will
allow time travel.

**CHECK
THE BOOK**

In *The Human
Touch* (2006), Frayn
considers many
physical and
metaphysical issues
relevant to *Spies*.
In 'Grand theatre'
(pp. 111–38), he
discusses the use of
a time machine to
revisit one's earlier
self – a function for
which he uses
memory and
imagination in
Spies.

This blurs the distinction between what 'really happened' and what is imagined. It reminds us that we are reliant within the fiction on Stephen's shaky and uncertain memories of events. And it reminds us that, outside the **metafiction** of Stephen's recollections, the whole narrative is made up by the novelist. Life in the Close after Mrs Hayward's arrest is as vividly depicted as normal life in the Close – and why not? Both are equally possible.

Occasionally, something is so improbable that it cannot be imagined. This helps Stephen to sort out possible scenarios and future actions. He considers telling a policeman that Mrs Hayward is a spy, but 'the words will not imagine themselves' (Ch. 3, p. 54).

Just as his sensory memory is good, Stephen's imagination extends into all his senses, too. He feels the coffin pressing down on him, and when thinking about the kisses that Auntie Dee may have exchanged with a lover, it is as a scent that he is aware of it: 'the ghost of those stolen kisses, lingered like a faint scent in the air' (Ch. 7, p. 141), recalling that it was the scent of privet that drew Stefan on his pilgrimage in the first place.

THE NATURE OF KNOWLEDGE

As in so many cases, knowledge is power in *Spies*. Stephen unwittingly gains power over Mrs Hayward by the knowledge that he garners from his and Keith's spying activity. He is embarrassed by the reversal this creates since he leans heavily on social order to give him a sense of security and to direct his actions. In turn, knowledge gives Barbara Berrill power over Stephen. Her knowledge is superior to Stephen's on many topics including sexual activity and local gossip, and as a consequence she can easily intimidate and embarrass him. It is all the more humiliating for Stephen because she is a girl. He pretends to know things that he does not in order not to let too much power slip away from him. Keith manipulates Stephen by leading him to think that he, Stephen, knows more than Keith does, then turning the tables on him. This is another of his methods of keeping Stephen cowed and reinforces Stephen's belief in Keith's superior intelligence.

With knowledge, also, comes loss of innocence. The harmless game of spying becomes treacherous and serious once the boys uncover real secret knowledge. Sexual knowledge is part of growing up, and Stephen is just beginning to acquire it. As soon as he does, he also recognises his own mortality and sees the path ahead not as 'remote blue horizons' (Ch. 8, p. 167) but as 'even darker tunnels' (Ch. 9, p. 180).

Occasionally, Stefan digresses into an **epistemological** consideration of what it means to know or understand something. These philosophical explorations are not very rigorous, and add little to our understanding of the issues at hand. It becomes clear that Stefan believes he both knew that the man in the Barns was not a German and still believed him to be so in some sense. It is similar to the way that a child can choose to believe in Father Christmas at the same time as knowing, rationally, that his or her parents must provide the presents. In philosophical terms, this is antimony – the concurrent acceptance of two mutually incompatible laws or beliefs. In literary terms, it is the willing suspension of disbelief that Samuel Taylor Coleridge (1772–1834) says is required of us in order to read literature, and particularly fiction. As readers, we are choosing to make the same leap of faith as Stephen – we know that really this has all been made up by Frayn, but we choose to believe, for the duration of our reading of the book, that the events really happened and that the narrator is recalling an actual history for us. In the same way, Stephen and Keith are making up a story about Mrs Hayward, as they have made up stories about Mr Gort and the ape-man, and choosing to believe in it.

The gulf between what characters think they know and what is actually true is often very great. But there is also a gulf between what we think we know and what is actually the case. The boys believe that Mrs Hayward is a spy and that the man at the Barns is a German or a tramp or both. We enjoy a feeling of superiority, believing we know that Mrs Hayward's 'suspicious' activity is completely innocent and that there is no German pilot. But it emerges that there is a grain of truth in their beliefs and we are wrong after all: Mrs Hayward does go on secret missions and she

QUESTION

The reviewer Hugo Barnacle finds Stephen implausibly credulous. Commenting on Stephen's co-existing beliefs that Keith's mother both is and is not a German spy, he says, 'surely even a ten-year-old knows better than that' (*New Statesman*, 4 February 2002). What do you think?

CHECK THE BOOK

Biographia Literaria (1817) by the **Romantic poet** Samuel Taylor Coleridge is an autobiographical discourse with philosophical digressions. The subtitle of the work is 'Biographical sketches of my literary life and opinions'. In it, Coleridge sets out his ideas and beliefs about literature.

CHECK THE BOOK

Michael Frayn's play *Copenhagen* (1998) deals with complex matter from theoretical physics, illustrated by the uncertainty principle put forward by Werner Heisenberg. Frayn has said that it approaches a question he finds crucial: 'How we know why people do what they do, and even how one knows what one does oneself ... The uncertainty principle says that there is no way, however much we improve our instruments, that we can ever know everything about the behaviour of a physical object. And I think it's also true about human thinking' (interview with Robyn Williams, ABC, 1 December 2001, to mark centenary of Heisenberg's birth).

does succour a pilot; the man at the Barns is a pilot, though not a German pilot who has been shot down.

As the novel deals with a **mystery**, knowledge that is slowly revealed is essential to its structure. But there is a lot which is not revealed to us until the last chapter, when Stefan fills in some background. We then realise that whatever we thought about the foregoing action must now be reassessed in the light of new knowledge. Frayn has recreated in us the same confidence in deduced knowledge that we have observed in the characters of the novel. In a sense, he does what Keith does to Stephen when he lets him think he is ahead in working out what is happening but has actually already got to the destination and is enjoying watching Stephen struggle or go off on the wrong tack: 'He's not behind me at all – he's somehow ahead of me again, and simply biding his time to tantalize me' (Ch. 3, p. 50). We are disturbed to find that our own confidence has been misplaced and may feel that the **narrator** is smirking over his final revelations. Is Frayn turning the joke on his readers? The twist at the end returns us to the question posed in the middle of the novel: 'What is it to know something?', 'What do I understand?' (Ch. 7, p. 138).

The method of acquiring knowledge that is practised throughout the novel is deduction from observation. Spying, which also means seeing, involves the **characters** in watching carefully and deducing situation and motives from what they observe. The unreliability of the method is highlighted in Chapter 8 when Barbara Berrill and Stephen both observe the same events, as Mrs Hayward and her husband walk to the post box, but come up with radically different interpretations of what they see (see **Extended commentaries: Text 1**). Yet working out what events mean just by watching them is exactly what the narrator is attempting to do and what we as readers have to do. The narrator is not giving us any reliable insights into the characters' inner states. He does not appear to have any such insights himself. Instead, he (and we) watch the action unfurl as though it were a film, sometimes zooming in to observe details and sometimes seeing flashbacks (the rusting croquet hoops on Auntie Dee's lawn, or – further back – the bombing of Miss Durrant's house). All we have to go in is what the narrator shows us. But

this is not enough unless we are very, very careful observers. The final chapter comes as a surprise. We are unlikely to have realised that Mr Wheatley is German, and that the family is Jewish. We cannot have guessed that he works in intelligence – that he is the German spy (though a spy who is German rather than a spy working for Germany). By undermining the deductive method of the novel in this way, Frayn leaves us uncertain what to believe at the end. It seems that we cannot be trusted to work things out for ourselves and must have all revealed to us by the narrator. This narrator, who seems to know so little about his characters, must suddenly be trusted as though he had always worn the robe of **omniscient narrator**. We don't trust him, we have no way of questioning him. In the end, all our knowledge is only partial and contingent.

LANGUAGE

NARRATIVE STYLE

Spies is written in an informal, conversational style. The **first-person narrator** makes frequent interjections, and sometimes intrusions, into the sequence of the narrative. He seems to be talking to himself a lot of the time as he struggles to remember what happened. Many passages appear to present his **stream of consciousness** rather than the carefully worked out prose we may expect from the narrator of a novel. For example, he says something about a jug of lemonade, then begins the next paragraph with 'No, wait. I've got that wrong' (Ch. 2, p. 31). This is a **conceit** – it is not that Frayn really stumbled over the words or sequence, but that he is giving his narrator a hesitant voice and punctuating his narrative with pauses, corrections and digressions to make points about his character, about the themes of memory and knowledge, and about how stories are constructed. He could have struck out the bit that was wrong – the assertion that the jug was on the tea table – and left only the corrected statement, that it was outside. By leaving the error and the narrator's train of thought, Frayn reinforces the idea that the narrator is struggling to recall the details of the story.

QUESTION

The critic Michiko Kakutani has said that Frayn uses 'the voice of the older Stephen to comment on the action, much the way a voice-over might be used in a movie' ('That nice lady up the road. A spy?', *New York Times*, 9 April 2002). Discuss the cinematographic qualities of *Spies*.

CONTEXT

The title, *Spies*, refers to Stephen and Keith spying on Mrs Hayward, but also to many other spies or possible spies in the novel. Stephen and Keith believe that Mrs Hayward is a spy; Stephen at one point claims that his father is a spy; Keith claims that his father works for the Secret Service; Stephen's own father really does work in military intelligence; Barbara Berrill spies on Stephen and Keith; there are rumours of a peeping Tom spying on women in the Close.

One of the most striking aspects of the style of *Spies* is the use of the present tense to describe things that happened in the past. This has the effect of giving the historical narrative immediacy and suggesting that the narrator is seeing or experiencing again the events he describes. It is as though he watches events unfold before him, rather like watching a film of his own past. By relating the plot in the present tense, too, the narrator is able to build tension and engage our sympathy. We feel things as Stephen feels them, and we discover things at the same pace as he does. Even if, with the benefit of a mature point of view, we can see what is coming we are able to experience everything alongside Stephen. This is encouraged by the **narrator**, who never uses the benefit of hindsight to tell us how things will work out or what will happen next. By using a narrator who cannot clearly remember events, and who is apparently uncovering them at the same rate that he is telling them, Frayn allows us to accompany both Stephen and Stefan on a voyage of discovery.

The narrator often refers to his younger self as Stephen, describing events as though they have happened to someone else. At other times, he refers to 'I' and 'we' (meaning him and Keith). Generally, the narrator refers to Stephen as 'I' in more intense passages and when he is more certain of what happened or how he felt. He refers to Stephen in the third person when there is less emotional intensity and when he understands less well what he was thinking or feeling at the time. Because the novel is more intense in later chapters, the use of the first person is more frequent towards the end of the novel. Perhaps, too, Stefan is feeling closer to his young self and more confident of his **narrative** once he has walked around the Close and become engaged with his story.

The locations in the novel all have generic, descriptive names: the Close, the Avenue, the Barns, the Cottages and the Lanes. This makes it impossible to locate the story precisely, but gives it a sense of both ordinariness and universality. The Close could be any middle-class estate built in the 1930s. The implication is that events like these could have happened anywhere; everywhere, domestic dramas and tragedies happen to ordinary people and are hidden behind the serene façade of similar households and neighbourhoods.

The message is that it is nothing special, and yet it is all special – it is not extraordinary, but events like these have a huge impact on the people they involve.

Language is important as a theme, as well as being the vehicle for communicating the novel. The older Stefan has made his career out of using language, but the younger Stephen is particularly inarticulate. He is often tongue-tied or silent. This reduces the potential for a conflict of voices; it is the voice of the older man that predominates at all times. Misunderstanding words is a running joke in the novel. In this way, language is set up as a barrier to understanding – the direct opposite of its function as a means of communication.

Language provides the only way for the narrator to present his own perspective or commentary since he has renounced more direct methods. Stefan denies any privileged knowledge because, he claims, his memory is faulty. We are going to see the history through Stephen's eyes. The narrator adopts the point of view of the young boy in telling the story, but succeeds at the same time in conveying his adult perspective on events through his use of language. Instead of explicit comment, he uses **irony** to suggest an alternative interpretation. He often presents Stephen's view in such a way that we know he is directing us to disagree with it. So, when he says of Keith '[h]is authority was entirely warranted by his intellectual and imaginative superiority' (Ch. 2, p. 16), we know that this is not true. Keith has not demonstrated any intellectual superiority. Even if he had, this would not give him the right to dominate Stephen. The point of the statement is to make us disagree with it and so conclude that there is no valid reason for Stephen to cede authority to Keith – it is a demonstration of his compliant **character** and Keith's domineering personality.

IMAGERY AND SYMBOLISM

Meanings cluster around a few repeated **symbols** or **leitmotifs** in Spies. The most important of these is privet. It represents the clipped, mannered society of the suburbs, with its rank, hypnotic smell standing for the hidden unpleasantnesses and wildness concealed by that society. There is something at once appealing and

CONTEXT

Frayn has said of the difficulties of capturing the real world in writing: 'that is the difficulty of the world from the point of the writer. It's not in words. It's tree-shaped and cloud-shaped and room-shaped. It's not word-shaped' (**http:// writersalmanac. publicradio.org**, 8 September 2002).

CONTEXT

Privet is not only pungent but also toxic. The leaves are poisonous, and landscape gardeners wear protective clothes and masks when cutting privet hedges to avoid the noxious fumes from its cut leaves and branches.

NARRATIVE TECHNIQUE AND STRUCTURE

...here is lo... source of... comedy, a... of language. Te co... childish perspective in sophistic... naivety. The existence of humour in th... the seriousness of its concerns or the events... many examples of humour, often in the form of in... moments of heightened tension or emotional intensity. ... to destroy the mood. It can be frustrating for us as readers, but... communicates the narrator's continuing discomfort with anything too emotional.

Some of the humour is directed at Stephen, but is never vicious. Often, the effect is to underline endearingly childish aspects of his character and to create distance between the adult narrator and child protagonist. When Mrs Hayward is in the hideout, Stephen is overcome by embarrassment. It is made worse when she mentions the sign that says 'privet'. At the sound of the word, which he thinks shameful, coming from her lips, he reddens. He wonders if she doesn't know what the word means, but then she says, 'Awful smell it's got in summer', and he thinks, 'No, she does know' (Ch. 5, p. 106). We smile at his embarrassment, and at him not knowing what the word means, and then again at his misunderstanding of the word. The ongoing joke about privet and privies is the kind of toilet humour that young boys enjoy, and this adds an extra dimension to Frayn's turning the joke on Stephen.

...his original misunderstanding her comment about the smell so that it reinforces...

...ents that form the main plot of Spies take place during the ...World War, but woven around these events is the journey of ...r to the place where he grew up. As he reflects on what ...xty years before, we see events obliquely, mediated ...stant memory. The narrator's frequent intrusions

CONTEXT

Stephen's misunderstanding of 'Jews', which he refers to as 'the Juice' (Ch. 2, p. 16), is humorous. It reminds us that he is comparatively ignorant outside his immediate social circle. It recalls a similar confusion of the name 'Hugh' and the word 'you' in The Go-Between.

CONTEXT

Some of Frayn's plays are **farces**, and are wholly focused on the absurdity to be observed in human behaviour.

IMAGERY AND SYMBOLISM continued

CONTEXT

Adam Mars-Jones sees privet in the novel as 'an emblem of a way of life with plenty of hidden strangeness, a rawness under the tranquillity' ('Spies like us', *The Observer*, 10 February 2002).

CONTEXT

The King James or Authorised Version of the Bible is the translation of the Bible which was used almost universally in Britain from the time of its publication in 1611 until the publication of the New English Bible in 1961–70. The poetic language of the King James Version is preferred by many people and is emulated by Stefan (Ch. 3, p. 53).

---

sickening about the scent, as there is about t...
public view – in this novel they include do...
affairs, treachery and desertion. Another...
letter 'x', which stands for all kinds of v...
represent Stephen's state of ignorance...

The trains, present mostly as sound...
suggesting a link with the outside...
the isolation of this small comm...
Uncle Peter, who is physically...
his desertion, is most closely...
Hayward is also connected...
within her abusive marria...
Uncle Peter.

There is much religio...
This ranges from th...
comparison betw...
p. 25) and the b...
p. 55) to more...
Creation in...
instantly b...
the Englis...
brought their a...
words became so' (C...
alone to the Barns he is 'exp...
weaknesses. The word is usually u...
sins and its resonance creates a fleeting...
pilgrimage, a religious journey undertaken to...
itemisation of the landmarks as he passes them recalls...
a pilgrimage. The boys' belief that the mystery has a Germa...
connection is central to all that Stephen does and he struggles to
hold on to it in the face of counter-evidence. The narrator says: 'It
remained, like some residual belief in God amidst a sea of doubt
about the theological details, the one sure item of faith that Stephen
had to hold on to' (Ch. 7, p. 140). The extravagance of the religious
imagery clustering around the adventure serves to demonstrate how
important it was to Stephen at the time, but is also humorous, as it is
clearly a ridiculous comparison.

NARRATIVE TECHNIQUE AND STRUCTURE

serve to distance the action set in the past. Often, a solid as w...ue
fully engaged with events, the narrator reminds us of his presen...
and the framework of the story set in the past, however much we may
get carried along by the story set in the past. The narrator can be seen as irritating at
times, with his pedantic uncertainty and persistent undermining of
the storyline. The effect, *ironically*, is to increase our desire for
engagement as we want to push the narrator aside, as it were, and
watch the story unfold.

The early part of the novel moves slowly as we follow the path of
the often fruitless spying activity of Stephen and Keith, and not
much happens. Tension starts to build when we realise that Mrs
Hayward really does have a secret of some kind. It then grows
slowly over the middle of the book as the pressure on Stephen and
our interest in Mrs Hayward increase. Much of the tension comes
from Stephen's inner state, creating a sense of claustrophobia. The
claustrophobia is emphasised by the action taking place in enclosed
spaces – the hideout, the tunnel, the dark of Stephen's bedroom, Mr
Hayward's garage and the 'living grave' at the Barns.

Very little is seen head-on in *Spies*. Just as Stephen and Keith spy on
the action in the Close, we are left in much the same position –
spying on the action, as it were, and trying to work out what is
happening from incomplete information. Everything is hedged
around with doubt, screened, hidden, misunderstood, hinted at;
events take place in the dark, or when Stephen is not there to
witness them. It is as if the whole action of the novel is seen out of
the corner of the eye. This technique also increases the tension for
readers because we are anxious to find out what is going on. The
tension increases rapidly towards the end of the novel, as events
pile up and quickly run out of control. The final chapters bring a
great rush of action and emotion.

The framing *narrative* is unbalanced in the same way as the...
historical narrative. At the start, the narrator sets out his d...
think about his past, but gives us minimal information a...
himself and creates little sense of urgency. The end of t...
though, brings a mass of new detail and the twist tha...

QUESTION

Consider how important the different state of childhood in the 1940s is to the novel.

QUESTION

In *Headlong*, the narrator says as he looks at a painting: 'The human eye sees very little at any one moment ... what I'm seeing at any one moment, really seeing, is a patch of paint about an inch in diameter. I'm seeing one tiny detail.' How could this statement be applied to *Spies*?

re-evaluate all that has gone before. The surprise revelation undermines the identification of the narrator with Stephen the boy. Suddenly, he has a different name and belongs to the groups that he has derided and feared – Jews and Germans. The narrator now appears to be manipulative. At the very least, he seems unaware of his duties to furnish us with the facts necessary to understanding his story. It appears that the whole thing has been a game, this time perpetrated by the narrator against us. Only when '[t]he game's finally over' (Ch. 10, p. 222) does he show his hand and reveal the trick he has played on us.

CONTEXT

Talking of his plays, Michael Frayn has said: 'I've always had what is no doubt a character failing … of wanting to keep everything nicely smoothed over in life: of not wanting anyone to make any difficulties or whatever. Left to myself, without reflection, I would probably write a play in which people just said very nice things to each other … theatre needs slightly more conflict than that, [so] I tend to have characters coming on saying there are terrible things going on out there, fighting and what have you … But it's still off-stage' (interview with Mark Lawson, 'Have I retired? It's hard to know', *The Guardian*, 3 May 2006).

PART FOUR

CRITICAL HISTORY

Spies is a recent novel (2002) and there has not been time for a body of critical discussion to have built up around it. However, it was reviewed extensively when it was published, providing a source of direct comment on the themes, structure and success of the novel.

Reviewers have noted the interest in memory and imagination which Frayn develops in the novel, and looked at the narratorial voice and the stance the **narrator** takes in relation to Stephen. There is general agreement that Frayn recreates the perspective of a young boy convincingly. There is less agreement over how well he paces the story and whether the ending is a masterstroke or something of a disappointment.

Adam Mars-Jones, reviewing *Spies* in *The Observer*, comments on how Frayn sets up two perspectives within the novel – that of Stefan and of Stephen – and then deliberately fails to deliver the insights an older narrator could give. 'This can seem a rather perverse piece of construction, setting up a double perspective and then muffling it, but its great virtue is that it shuts out whimsy' ('Spies like us', *The Observer*, 10 February 2002). He points out that it allows Stefan to 'fret over' the past 'without claiming authority over it'. At the same time, it allows Frayn to recreate and respect Stephen's point of view without being limited by it. Hugo Barnacle, writing in the *New Statesman* (4 February 2002), finds the double perspective unconvincing: 'One can see the double-vision effect Frayn is trying for, but it doesn't quite come off.' He also feels that the novel 'suffers from a major drawback in the area of plausibility'.

Mars-Jones finds Frayn's forays into **epistemology** unconvincing and unsatisfying – he calls them 'strained passages, ponderings with a whiff of the seminar, rather too methodical for the context'. In particular, he thinks the ending, which strays into mysticism, is unjustified in a story 'in which individual patches of knowledge and ignorance are fitted into a fully coherent pattern. In fact, the whole underlying principle of the book's construction is that there is no such single thing as knowing, an on/off state like a light switch.'

 QUESTION

One critic has asked 'Precisely how tragic, and how comic, is all this supposed to be?' To what extent can *Spies* be called either comic or tragic?

CONTEXT

The study of knowledge is a branch of philosophy called epistemology. In Plato's *Theaetetus*, Socrates sets out several possible definitions of knowledge. That which has been most influential, and widely accepted until it was contested in the 1960s, is that knowledge is a 'justified true belief'.

John Lanchester describes the novel as 'a study of the difference between what we think we know and what is real, and also of the difference between what we really know and what we are prepared to admit' (*New York Review of Books*, June 2002).

Peter Bradshaw ('Children's crusade', *The Guardian*, 9 February 2002) is one of the few critics who find the ending of *Spies* wholly satisfactory, comparing the last fifty pages to pulling back the joystick in a plane like Uncle Peter's to soar into literary acrobatics. Even so, he calls it 'curious' that Frayn spends so long at a sauntering pace setting up the novel before this rapid and showy **denouement**. Paul Bailey ('Lost in the smoke of wartime memories', *The Independent*, 16 February 2002) finds it 'deftly plotted' but that there 'are almost too many revelations in the final pages'. John Updike, too, feels that 'slightly too much seems to happen toward the end, abetted by too many artfully delayed recognitions' ('Absent presences', *New Yorker*, 1 April 2002). Max Watman finds it even less satisfactory, particularly in that we have to wait so long for information which Stefan had in his possession at the start: 'The unnecessary and empty suspense can't jibe with Frayn's insistence that the book be cast as a recollection. The same is true for the willful naïveté of the child narrator. If we are not to benefit from the older man's perspective until the last dozen or so pages, why introduce him at the start?' ('Guileless games', *New Criterion*, May 2002). Michiko Kakutani is similarly unimpressed by Frayn's 'coy refusal' to reveal facts which Stefan has at his fingertips from the beginning. He finds the book ending on 'a decidedly unconvincing note' that feels 'contrived' and 'ham-handed'. It is, he says, a 'hokey, expository conclusion' that undermines our trust in the narration ('That nice lady up the road. A spy?', *New York Times*, 9 April 2002).

QUESTION

Do you find the ending of *Spies* satisfactory? How well do you think it works in terms of the pace and progression of the rest of the novel?

SPIES AND CRITICAL MOVEMENTS

The main movements in critical theory during the course of the twentieth century have been from **modernism** to **postmodernism**, incorporating **structuralism**, **post-structuralism** and **deconstructionist** theory. Parts of the postmodernist movement,

such as **Marxist** and **feminist** criticism, concentrate on particular social angles in literature and its relationship to culture or society.

MODERNISM AND POSTMODERNISM

Modernism, broadly, encompasses the unorthodox or experimental. Modernist fiction often dispenses with the linear 'realistic' plot which formed the mainstay of nineteenth-century fiction and moved to a more fragmented approach to presenting experience. Modernist writers tend to concentrate on mediating personal experience using experimental **narrative** methods and forms, often focusing on the alienation of the individual by society's structures, restrictions and expectations. While modernism overturns the ordered structure of the nineteenth-century novel it does still intend to find and explore intricate, well ordered structures of its own. Postmodernism, on the other hand, denies any order and allows unity to dissolve into fragments. Various meanings may emerge from the different organisation of these fragments, and by looking at elements in different juxtapositions.

 **CHECK THE BOOK**
A good, general guide to reading novels using the tools of modern criticism is *Narrative Form* by Suzanne Keen (Palgrave, 2003). It gives a thorough survey of different approaches.

This perspective is useful to bear in mind because *Spies* is not a purely linear novel. It has an outer framework or **metafiction** set in the near present in which it was written (around the new millennium), yet it recounts events set in the early 1940s through a series of flashbacks. The narrative moment moves between the 1940s and 'nearly sixty years' later. There is, too, a constant feeling of uncertainty about what happened, when and why. The **narrator** has an unreliable memory, and the events are long in the past.

The outer fiction has a linear narrative of its own in which the old man revisits the scene of his childhood and tries to rebuild in his memory what happened. This is consistent and is not seriously undermined, but it is not tidily resolved. The narrative framework is of a journey, both into the past and into a different country. But it is a journey with a beginning and a middle but no end: after his trip down 'Memory Lane', Stefan doesn't know where to go and still feels rootless and unsettled.

Within this narrative framework we observe the reconstruction of Stephen's story. The narrator struggles to make a linear narrative,

but his material is elusive and won't easily fit the shape that he wants. The narrator tries to place the visits of the policeman in time but is unsure where they fall or if there were two visits or one. He can't quite remember when Uncle Peter visited, or whether the events took place in spring or summer. By forcing himself into the foreground as he presents his struggle and process, he fractures the narrative further. He is an old-fashioned man, trying to make an old-fashioned story, but the story is having none of it and proves to be as unruly as his memory.

The French critic, philosopher and theorist Roland Barthes (1915–80) divides texts into those that are 'readerly' and those that are 'writerly' (though a text may be both). A writerly text involves readers in creating its meaning, requiring them to reflect on the method of its composition and the relation of its parts, to make choices and decisions and interpret rather than being restricted by a single meaning imposed by a dictatorial author. A readerly text presents its own agenda firmly and does not invite contradiction or the engagement of the reader in making the text. At the end of *Spies* 'all the mysteries are resolved, or as resolved as they're ever likely to be' (Ch. 11, p. 234). Both the level of **resolution** achieved and the evaluation of this resolution are decided by the narrator – we are not invited to question his verdict. Indeed, our role has been to be carried along not only by the narrative but by a deceitful narrator who has allowed us (like Stephen led by Keith) to think that we are ahead of the game, but then to find that he has the real answer up his sleeve. Even so, the narrator has not entirely succeeded, and in the gap between his ambition and his achievement there is a readerly space for reflection. In being 'as resolved as they're ever likely to be' the mysteries remain partly unresolved. Resolution has, finally, eluded him: the story won't be tied down to fulfil a purpose and it escapes from its maker.

Whether or not *Spies* was written as a postmodernist text would not bother a postmodernist critic. Postmodernist criticism does not require the meanings discovered in a text to have been put there deliberately by the author, but elevates the role of the reader and endorses their response, following the lead of **reader-response** theory propounded by Wolfgang Iser (1926–2007). There are many

 **CHECK THE BOOK**

A good text on postmodernism is Ian Gregson's *Postmodernist Literature* (Arnold, 2004).

CONTEXT

Roland Barthes worked with the idea that the meaning of a signifier, whether a word, **icon** or image, is culturally determined and redetermined. In *Mythologies* (1957), he explores how meaning is fixed on icons to promote or communicate bourgeois values, often in contradiction to more obvious or logical meanings. The adoption of privet in middle-class gardens, despite its rank smell, could be analysed in this way.

FEMINIST CRITICISM

Feminist criticism looks at the representation of women in literature and the way this reflects and mediates social attitudes towards women. The only developed female characters in *Spies* are Mrs Hayward and Barbara Berrill. Mrs Hayward is dominated physically by her husband. At home, she has no freedom at all. She is shown as a languid, elegant woman who enjoys a leisured life – this in itself makes her something of a 'trophy wife' and disempowers her. But below the surface it is worse still. The only personal incidents recorded in her diary are related to her sexual function as Mr Hayward's wife and her domestic function as wife and mother. Mr Hayward rules over her with complete authority and inflicts physical suffering on her when she challenges his authority or displeases him. She has a secret life in which she breaks the rules of marriage and society – but this is wrecked (unwittingly) by the actions of young boys. She has to abase herself before Stephen to plead with him to take the basket to the Barns, and a feminist critic might object, too, that her relationship with Uncle Peter consists of the same sorts of domestic service – obtaining provisions and mending and washing clothes – as she is obliged to perform for her husband and son.

On the other hand, Barbara Berrill is an example of the feminine as yet untrammelled by the expectations and restrictions of society. She lures Stephen into smoking, she takes the initiative in their first sexual encounters and she belongs to an all-female household said to be 'running wild' with no man to control them. Barbara represents alluring yet rather scary (for Stephen) unbridled femininity. He associates her with freedom, wildness, chaos and trouble – and he is sorry to lose her when she turns her affections to Dave Avery. She is the antithesis of Mrs Hayward. It would not be lost on a feminist critic that Stephen is undiscerning in his attraction to the feminine – he has awkward sexual feelings towards both of them. Barbara is emasculatingly scary. His encounter with her is a parody of a rape with her finally wrestling Mrs Hayward's letter from him. With Mrs Hayward, he has an embarrassing awareness of her bosom and her softness. Her femininity appeals to him, though he cannot admit it to himself.

QUESTION

What is the role of the female characters in *Spies*? How are they represented?

QUESTION

The sculptor Michelangelo (1475–1564) claimed that his role was to release the angel from the stone, not to create it. Does the **narrator** of *Spies* similarly refuse to take responsibility for his creation?

PART FIVE

BACKGROUND

MICHAEL FRAYN'S LIFE AND WORK

Michael Frayn was born in a North London suburb on 8 September 1933. His early childhood was very happy, but this came to an end with the sudden death of his mother from a heart attack when Frayn was twelve years old. He and his sister were not allowed to go to their mother's funeral, and never spoke of her again after her death. Frayn's father, a deaf asbestos salesman, could no longer afford Michael's school fees and removed him from his exclusive public school, placing him in Kingston Grammar School. Frayn endured a miserable four or five years which ended when he was around sixteen and made strong friendships and discovered literature and music. It was, he says, 'like the sun coming out from behind a very black cloud' (interview with John Tusa, BBC Radio 3, 4 April 2004).

During his time doing National Service in 1952–4, Frayn was sent to the Joint Services School for Linguists in Cambridge to learn Russian. Afterwards he stayed in Cambridge, studying Modern Languages (French and Russian) and then Moral Sciences (philosophy) at Emmanuel College of the University of Cambridge.

After Cambridge, Frayn joined *The Guardian* (then named the *Manchester Guardian*) in 1957. He worked for the paper as a columnist from 1959 to 1962, moving to work at *The Observer* from 1962 to 1968. After formally leaving *The Observer*, he has continued to contribute occasionally to both *The Observer* and *The Guardian*. Four volumes of his collected columns have been published.

Frayn has written plays, novels, three screenplays, an operetta and a book of philosophical essays (*The Human Touch*, 2006). He has also made a series of programmes for BBC TV about different places, including the London where he grew up.

> **CONTEXT**
>
> Frayn's play *Make and Break* (1980) is about a salesman of building materials.

> **CONTEXT**
>
> During the period 1949–60, all able-bodied men in the UK had to serve two years of compulsory military service, called National Service. On leaving school, a young man had to join the Army, Air Force or Navy. Frayn's training in Russian was intended to equip him for military intelligence work.

His first play to be staged, *The Two of Us* (1970), was savaged by critics, but his subsequent farce, *Donkeys' Years* (1976), was very successful. He has written more than twenty plays, including the other highly successful farce, *Noises Off* (1982), and the more serious *Copenhagen* (1998), about a meeting during the Second World War between two scientists (one a German, the other half-Jewish) Werner Heisenberg and Nils Bohr, and *Democracy* (2003), about a spy scandal during Willy Brandt's term as Chancellor of Germany. He has also translated plays by Russian writers Anton Chekhov and Leo Tolstoy and the French writer Jean Anouilh.

His novels include *The Tin Men* (1965), *Towards the End of the Morning* (1967) and *Headlong* (1999), about a man who believes his neighbour has a valuable unidentified painting by Breugel and determines to get it from him. *Headlong* was shortlisted for the Booker Prize in 1999; *The Tin Men* won the Somerset Maugham Award in 1965.

Frayn is married to the biographer Claire Tomalin and lives in Surrey, England.

LITERARY BACKGROUND

Spies can be related to several strands in literary and popular fiction. It is an **historical novel**, since the main part of the action is set in the past in a specifically identified historical period. In particular, it is a war story and borrows from the tradition in children's literature of boys' adventure stories. It also has aspects of the **coming-of-age novel** – a genre in which the struggles and transitions of a character going through adolescence are explored – and includes elements of **mystery**.

WAR STORIES

War stories are a particular subset of historical novels. There have been novels, plays and poems written about the First and Second World Wars. Some of the popular fiction and films written soon after the Second World War glorified the war and the role of the combatants. Even during the war, Stephen could have read comics

that presented tales of war heroism and adventure (see below). Popular presentations of the war made while it was ongoing were often jingoistic and propagandist.

Other depictions of the war, particularly those written some time later, are more thoughtful and honest. The presentation of the war that comes at the end of *Spies*, with Uncle Peter's moving account of what happened to him and the vignette of Stefan's aunt dying in her cellar with her children, belongs in this category. It overturns the naive view demonstrated earlier through Stephen's perspective.

BOYS' OWN ADVENTURES

Boys' adventure stories of the type that Stephen and Keith might have read themselves lend something to *Spies*. This type of tale, sometimes called 'Boys' Own' adventures after *Boys' Own Paper*, was popular reading with young boys in the first half of the twentieth century. Other boys' comics that were popular at the time *Spies* is set (and Frayn was a boy) were *Gem* and *Magnet*. The engagement of boys with the stories was considerable and enthusiastic, as George Orwell remarked at the time. The type of stories that featured in boys' comics and papers often tell of daring adventures in which boys are fearless heroes and accomplish great deeds, often in the context of nationalism. Stephen sometimes reflects on the glory and the responsibility that the quest to unmask a German spy entails. He romanticises their role and revels in their contribution to the war effort.

Keith is sometimes allowed to borrow adventure stories that belonged to Uncle Peter. The idealistic depiction of this character in the early part of the novel draws on fictional heroes such as Biggles, a fighter pilot created by W. E. Johns in the First World War who continued to have adventures between the wars, in the Second World War and in the Cold War after 1945. Other influences from Frayn's own childhood include the *Just William* stories by Richmal Crompton (1890–1969) and the adventure stories written by Arthur Ransome (1884–1967). In the *Just William* collections of short stories (from 1922), the eleven-year-old schoolboy William Brown and his friends enjoy various pranks and adventures. In the nineteenth book, *William the Showman* (1937), William hatches a

CHECK THE FILM

A film which shows graphically some of the horror of the Second World War is *Saving Private Ryan* (1998).

CONTEXT

Boys' Own Paper was first published in 1879. It was originally intended to encourage reading and Christian values among young boys. It featured puzzles, competitions, adventure stories and articles about heroes such as great sportsmen. The *Paper* ceased publication in 1967.

CHECK THE BOOK

W. E. Johns (1893–1968) wrote ninety-six Biggles novels. Johns was himself a fighter pilot in the First World War, and then started the magazine *Popular Flying* in which he first created the character of Biggles.

BOYS' OWN ADVENTURES continued

 CHECK THE NET

The novelist George Orwell (real name Eric Blair, 1903–50) wrote an article on the comics and papers read by boys in the war years and the period between the two World Wars, called *Boys' Weeklies* (1940). It is possible to find the essay online. Using a search engine search for 'Orwell' and 'Boys' weeklies'.

plan to catch spies. When his brother Robert ridicules his exploits, William wonders if this is because Robert is himself a spy. Arthur Ransome's *Swallows and Amazons* books (from 1930) follow the sailing adventures of a family of two girls and two boys.

COMING-OF-AGE NOVELS

The difficult transition between childhood and adulthood has produced a large body of fiction. **Coming-of-age** novels usually concentrate on a single, pivotal event which catalyses the growing-up process for the **protagonist**. Although *Spies* does not fall fully into this category, it certainly draws on the tradition. We watch Stephen as he thinks he is beginning to enter the 'darker tunnels and more elusive terrors' of maturity (Ch. 9, p. 180), as he begins to shoulder adult responsibilities and as he has to exercise personal strengths. We see the beginnings of an interest in sex, and his first experiment with a cigarette.

The coming-of-age novel is a large and sprawling genre, but there are a few novels in it which have particular relevance to *Spies*. The most important of these is *The Go-Between* by L. P. Hartley. The story is told by an elderly man, Leo, who decides to revisit a village and country house in Norfolk where a seminal event in his childhood marked the end of innocence for him. Like Stephen, Leo was a shy boy, socially inferior to his friend Marcus. He goes to stay at Marcus's country home in Norfolk during the hot summer of 1900. While he is there, he becomes embroiled in the affair between Marcus's sister Marian and a tenant farmer, Ted. Like Stephen, he has to carry messages (hence the title of the novel), and it is ultimately through his unwitting actions that the couple are discovered. As a result, Ted commits suicide. The older Leo has a diary that he kept during 1900, which helps him to reconstruct events. Like Stefan, he feels the need to visit the scene and try to lay ghosts. Again like Stefan, his life since has been rather dull and perhaps unsatisfactory. In Leo's case, the early exposure to a disastrous extramarital affair has had the result of putting him off romantic attachment, and he has never married. While Stefan wonders if Mrs Hayward is still alive, and fancies he sees Barbara Berrill, Leo seeks out and visits Marian in his quest for absolution. Both Leo and Stephen suffer terrible feelings of guilt at the part they

have played in the adult dramas acted out around them. Both are drawn in against their wishes and beyond their understanding. In both cases, their involvement begins as a boyish game but rapidly gets out of their control.

There are echoes, too, of William Golding's novel *Lord of the Flies* (1954). In this, a group of boys is stranded on a desert island in wartime (it may be the Second World War, or perhaps an imagined Third World War). The isolated space of the island is a microcosm of the world, in which the boys establish a primitive society with a quickly evolved body of myth. The boys' difficulties soon lead to terror and victimisation. One boy is killed, and most of the others are convinced there is a monster on the island. There is a pilot who has been shot down and killed; his parachute is mistaken for the beast. Golding's novel explores the barbarity that boys, particularly frightened boys, are capable of when outside the authority of adults, suggesting that this 'dark heart' exists in all people but is kept in check by civilisation. The private kingdom of Stephen and Keith in the hideout, where Keith rules as bully and maker of rules, recalls Golding's island. Like *Spies*, *Lord of the Flies* uses a series of **leitmotifs** (including a conch shell, the glasses worn by one of the boys and a severed pig's head).

MYSTERY

Mysteries are stories that revolve around a central puzzle, usually a crime and often a murder, which the **characters** have to solve during the course of the action. They are generally written in such a way that it is difficult for the reader confidently to solve the mystery much in advance of the **protagonists**, and the reader discovers clues at the same time as the protagonists. Frayn follows this pattern of revealing things to us only as they are revealed to Stephen, but he can achieve this only by having the **narrator** withhold crucial information until the very end of the story. Since Stefan is Stephen, and is in possession of the full facts at the start of his telling of the tale, his act of withholding information has been seen by some critics to be fraudulent, or a betrayal of the implicit contract between writer and reader (see **Critical history**).

Spies cannot be called a true mystery. First, except for Uncle Peter's

CONTEXT

John Updike has noted that much literature in which an older man returns to the scene of earlier events features a meeting and recognition, and *Spies* is unusual in that no such meeting occurs, frustrating our expectations. He cites early and late examples: Odysseus, recognised by his dog in the *Odyssey* (Homer, seventh or eighth century BC), and Captain Ryder, recognised by Nanny Hawkins in *Brideshead Revisited* (Evelyn Waugh, 1945).

CONTEXT

The first mystery is generally considered to be *The Murders in the Rue Morgue* by American author Edgar Allan Poe (1841). Like most mysteries, it relates to the solving of a murder – or, in this case, a series of murders.

QUESTION

Clare Tomalin said of her husband's novel *Spies*: 'It is one that will last and people will be reading it in 100 years time' (BBC Radio 4, 29 January 2003). Do you think *Spies* has qualities that will allow it to endure?

CHECK THE NET

For accounts and photographs of the Blitz and the war in England, go to **www.eyewltness tohistory.com**, **www.historyplace. com** and **www.bbc.co.uk**

desertion, there is no real crime in the novel. In addition, the mystery of what Mrs Hayward is doing has already been solved by the narrator before he begins to tell his tale. Many readers will have guessed that the man in the Barns is Uncle Peter, and that Mrs Hayward is romantically involved with him in some way, long before it becomes apparent through the unfolding of events to Stephen. Even so, *Spies* borrows many devices from the genre of the murder mystery, including the careful placing of clues which – at least in retrospect – lead us towards the true state of affairs.

HISTORICAL BACKGROUND

JEWISH PERSECUTION AND THE SECOND WORLD WAR

The Second World War broke out in September 1939 when the German forces under the direction of Adolf Hitler invaded Poland. Britain and France had an agreement to defend Poland and declared war on Germany on 3 September 1939. Other European powers quickly became involved. The German army was better organised and better equipped than the Allied (French, British and Polish) forces, and made rapid advances through mainland Europe. The German air force (*Luftwaffe*) was also better equipped than that of the Allied forces, with more modern planes that were strategically deployed to support the work of the ground-based forces.

The British mainland was never invaded, though air strikes took their toll on many English cities. London was bombed during the Blitz, an intensive bombing raid by the *Luftwaffe* which lasted from 7 September 1940 until 11 May 1941. The Blitz marked a change of tactic. Previously, Germany had targeted military installations in preparation for a planned invasion of Britain. By bombing civilian targets, the Nazis hoped to demoralise the British people to the point that they would surrender or agree terms with Germany. The British responded to the Blitz, as to the war as a whole, with a defiant spirit. A propaganda campaign to encourage women to work the land or in munitions factories, and to encourage everyone to grow their own food, live frugally, 'make do and mend' rather than demand new goods, and to contribute to the 'war effort' in every

way possible for the 'duration' of the war (both terms adopted by Stephen) was hugely successful.

In Germany, the Nazis began to persecute Jews in the 1930s. Hitler promoted the idea of a 'pure' race of Aryan Germans with blond hair and blue eyes. The Jews, with dark hair and dark eyes, were one of the groups that he wanted to exclude from German society. Jews have been persecuted throughout history for their religious beliefs. Often, persecution has focused on the financial acumen for which Jewish business people have become renowned. In Germany and Poland (under German rule), Jews were stripped of more and more civic and human rights. Beginning with prohibitions preventing Jews practising certain professions, the restrictions increased to prevent them holding land, running businesses and living where they pleased. Jews were forced to live in ghettos – areas of a city set aside for them alone. They were not allowed out after dark, had to wear distinctive clothing including an armband showing a yellow Star of David, and were robbed of their rights as citizens. Eventually, six million Jews around Europe were transported to concentration camps and murdered. It is against this background that Stefan's father is living in England, but is not revealing his Jewishness. Although Britain opposed Germany in the Second World War, there was little sympathy for Jews, particularly among the general populace.

SOCIAL SETTING

Social propriety was more of a concern in the 1940s than it is in modern Britain. People were encouraged to 'know their place' and social mobility was difficult. People from working families would be unlikely to go to university and unlikely to rise above the social station of their parents. Ambition was consequently limited for most people. There was no universal free health care, no council housing and little in the way of social benefit. Wealth was a measure of a person's success or – if it was inherited wealth – family background. The hierarchy of children in the Close reflects this strict zoning of society. Stephen comments that his family occupied one of the only pair of semi-detached houses and that the Pinchers,

> **CONTEXT**
>
> Mr Wheatley's dark hair is specifically mentioned in one of the few clues to Stephen's Jewish heritage.

> **CONTEXT**
>
> Of a Jewish population of 566,000 in Germany, 200,000 were killed. Of 3,300,000 Jews in Poland, three million were killed. Jews from France, Austria, Hungary, Czechoslovakia, Yugoslavia and Romania also fell victim to the Nazi purges.

CHECK THE NET

For a detailed account of the sequence of Nazi actions against the Jews in Europe, go to **www. historyplace.com** and follow the link to the Holocaust Timeline.

who occupied the other half, were 'even less desirable than we were, and the terrible connectedness of our houses brought us down with them' (Ch. 2, p. 12). To live in a detached house was the most respectable; a semi-detached house was less respectable. A terraced house was less respectable still, though there are none of these in the Close which is in a middle-class suburb of London. In the slums of major cities, the poorest people lived in back-to-backs – houses which were joined on three sides to other houses. These often had privies, the shared outside toilets which Stephen does not like to mention.

The awareness of social position which suffused adult society is well developed in Stephen. His strong feeling of social inferiority keeps him under Keith's spell as he is grateful to be allowed to be Keith's friend. He is entranced by the relative opulence of Keith's house. When he fantasises about a future in which Mrs Hayward has been arrested for spying, one of the sorrows he lists is that he will no longer be able to go for sumptuous teas at Keith's house. His admiration for Keith's house and the world it represents gives him the opportunity to itemise details of it and so helps to create the period setting so vividly for us. Although, to Stephen, Keith's family is the epitome of respectability, even he recognises that there is a yet more elevated station. Stephen and Keith find it inconceivable that Mrs Hayward might be visiting a house on the Avenue, an area occupied by higher-class families.

Stephen's phrase 'Thank you for having me', which becomes a **leitmotif**, is the ritual utterance every child had to make when leaving a house they had visited. For most children, it was repeated without feeling or much meaning, but Stephen genuinely is grateful for being allowed to visit and considers it an undeserved privilege. When he says it at the very end of the novel, it is his heartfelt farewell to the reader: 'thank you, everyone. Thank you for having me' (Ch. 11, p. 234).

Yet Stephen is not quite at the bottom of the social pecking order. The Pinchers are lower than him, and the children at the Cottages and in the Lanes are practically off the scale. It seems to him that they watch Stephen and Keith 'as if [they] were members of some

quite alien and incomprehensible race – Iron Age invaders in Stone Age territory, white settlers among aborigines' (Ch. 6, p. 126). His choice of comparison shows that he considers that they are superior to the children at the cottages: Iron Age people were more technologically and socially advanced than Stone Age people, and in the 1940s an English boy would have considered white settlers 'better' than Aborigines. When the possibility that Mrs Hayward has gone into a house in the Lanes is raised, Stephen says that they could not then pursue their project: 'Germans we might be able to deal with. These people we certainly can't' (Ch. 6, p. 127).

CHECK THE BOOK

Deadkidsongs by Toby Litt (2001) is another novel which explores the cruelty of which boys are capable. The story is set in the 1970s against the background of the Cold War. A group of boys plans heroic activities against the Russians whom they expect to invade. Their hideout is in a rhododendron hedge. When one of the boys dies of meningitis, the others decide it is the fault of his grandparents and set about killing the elderly couple. Like *Spies*, the novel tries to recreate childhood, and struggles with issues of the reliability of the narrator and the narrative.

World events

1914–18 First World War

1919 Treaty of Versailles establishes the grounds of peace after the First World War, limiting German military powers

1921 Adolf Hitler becomes leader of the National Socialist German Workers' Party

1933 Adolf Hitler becomes Chancellor of Germany and, soon after, dictator; first concentration camps open at Dachau, Buchenwald, Sachsenhausen and Ravensbrück to receive Jews; persecution of Jews begins as Nazis boycott Jewish shops and businesses, strip Jewish immigrants from Poland of German nationality and define Jews as 'non-Aryan'; Jews prohibited from owning land or editing newspapers

Author's life

1933 (8 September) Born in Mill Hill in London, England

Literary events

1908 First issue of the boys' magazine *The Magnet*; the magazine featured the Billy Bunter stories

1922 Publication of *Just William*, the first story about the character William Brown by Richmal Crompton (1890–1969)

1932 Publication of the first Biggles story in *Popular Flying* magazine; publication of the first book of Biggles stories, *The Camels are Coming*, by W. E. Johns (1893–1968)

World events	Author's life	Literary events
1934 Hitler becomes Führer on the death of German President Paul von Hindenberg		
1935 Nuremburg race laws against Jews declared, making it illegal for Jews to marry Aryan Germans and stripping Jews of their German citizenship		
1938 Jews have to register land, property and businesses		
1939 Curfew imposed on Jews; outbreak of the Second World War		
1940 Start of deportation of German Jews to Poland		**1940** Last issue of *The Magnet*
1941 Mass deportation of German Jews; beginning of mass killing of Jews in the 'Final Solution'		
		1942 Publication of the first Famous Five novel, *Five on a Treasure Island*, by Enid Blyton (1897–1968)
1945 End of Second World War; liberation of concentration camps; start of Nuremburg Trials to try Nazi war criminals; foundation of the Welfare State in Britain, resumption of house building		
	1946–51 Kingston Grammar School, London	
1948 Founding of the state of Israel; disappearance of the state of Palestine		

World events	Author's life	Literary events
		1949 Publication of *Death of a Salesman* by Arthur Miller (1915–2005)
	1952–4 During National Service, learns Russian at the Joint Services School for Linguists in Cambridge	
		1953 Publication of *The Go-Between* by L. P. Hartley (1895–1972)
	1954–7 Studies Modern Languages (French and Russian) and then Moral Sciences (philosophy) at Emmanuel College, University of Cambridge	**1954** Publication of *Lord of the Flies* by William Golding (1911–93)
	1956 Spends a month at Moscow University as one of the first foreign exchange students; the Russian students did not carry out their part of the exchange	
	1957 Starts work as a journalist on the *Manchester Guardian*	
1960 Arrest in Argentina of Adolf Eichmann, a senior Nazi responsible for persecution of Jews in Germany, Austria and Czechoslovakia		
1962 Execution of Adolf Eichmann for crimes against humanity and the Jewish people	**1962–8** Works as a regular columnist on *The Observer*	
	1965 Publication of first novel, *The Tin Men*; Somerset Maugham Award for *The Tin Men*	

World events	Author's life	Literary events
	1967 Publication of *Towards the End of the Morning* (novel)	
	1970 Production of first play in the West End, *The Two of Us*	
	1975 Production of *Alphabetical Order*; *London Evening Standard* Award for Best Comedy for *Alphabetical Order*	
	1976 Production of *Donkeys' Years* and Laurence Olivier Award for Best Comedy for *Donkeys' Years*	
		1981 Publication of *Goodnight Mr Tom* by Michelle Magorian (b. 1947)
	1982 Production of *Noises Off*; *London Evening Standard* Award for Best Comedy; Laurence Olivier Award for Best Comedy for *Noises Off*	
	1986 Release of first film, *Clockwise*, featuring John Cleese	
1988 Palestine Liberation Organisation declares the existence of the state of Palestine		
	1989 Screenplay for *First and Last*; allegedly declines a CBE	
	1990 International Emmy Award for *First and Last*	
	1991 Publication of A *Landing on the Sun* (novel)	

World events	Author's life	Literary events
	1998 Production of *Copenhagen*; Critics' Circle Award for Best New Play for *Copenhagen*; *London Evening Standard* Award for Best Play for *Copenhagen*	
	1999 Publication of *Headlong*; *Headlong* shortlisted for the Booker Prize	
		2001 Publication of *Atonement* by Ian McEwan (b. 1948)
	2002 Publication of *Spies*; Whitbread Best Novel Award for *Spies*; Whitbread Prize won by Claire Tomalin, Frayn's wife; Heywood Hill Literary Prize	
	2003 Commonwealth Writers Prize for Best Book (Eurasia Region) for *Spies*	
	2005 Honorary degree from the University of East Anglia	
	2006 Publication of *The Human Touch* (philosophy)	

WORKS BY MICHAEL FRAYN

The Day of the Dog, 1962 (articles from *The Guardian* newspaper)

The Book of Fub, 1963 (articles from *The Guardian* newspaper)

On the Outskirts, 1964 (articles from *The Guardian* newspaper)

The Tin Men, 1965 (novel)

The Russian Interpreter, 1966 (novel)

At Bay in Gear Street, 1967 (articles from *The Observer* newspaper)

Towards the End of the Morning, 1967 (novel)

A Very Private Life, 1968 (novel)

The Two of Us, 1970 (four one-act plays for two actors)

Sweet Dreams, 1973 (novel)

Constructions, 1974 (philosophy)

Alphabetical Order, 1977 (play)

Donkeys' Years, 1977 (play)

Clouds, 1977 (play)

Make and Break, 1980 (play)

Noises Off, 1982 (play)

Benefactors, 1984 (play)

Wild Honey, trans. Chekhov, 1984 (play)

Balmoral, 1987 (play)

The Trick of It, 1989 (novel)

First and Last, 1989 (play)

Jamie on a Flying Visit; and *Birthday*, 1990 (plays)

Listen to This: Sketches and Monologues, 1990 (play)

Look Look, 1990 (play)

A Landing on the Sun, 1991 (novel)

Audience, 1991 (play)

Here, 1993 (play)

La Belle Vivette, 1995 (adaptation of Jacques Offenbach's *La Belle Hélène*, play)

Now You Know, 1995 (play)

Speak After the Beep: Studies in the Art of Communicating with Inanimate and Semi-animate Objects, 1995 (articles from *The Guardian* newspaper)

Alarms and Excursions: More Plays than One, 1998 (play)

Copenhagen, 1998 (play)

Headlong, 1999 (novel)

Plays: Three, 2000 (play)

Celia's Secret: An Investigation (entitled *The Copenhagen Papers* in the USA), with David Burke, 2000 (non-fiction)

Spies, 2002 (novel)

Democracy, 2003 (play)

The Human Touch, 2006 (philosophy)

REVIEWS

Paul Bailey, 'Lost in the smoke of wartime memories', *The Independent*, 16 February 2002

Hugo Barnacle, *New Statesman*, 4 February 2002

Peter Bradshaw, 'Children's crusade', *The Guardian*, 9 February 2002

Michiko Kakutani, 'That nice lady up the road. A spy?', *New York Times*, 9 April 2002

John Lanchester, *New York Review of Books*, June 2002

Adam Mars-Jones, 'Spies like us', *The Observer*, 10 February 2002

John Updike, 'Absent presences', *New Yorker*, 1 April 2002

Max Watman, 'Guileless games', *New Criterion*, May 2002

BACKGROUND STUDIES

Malcolm Bradbury, *The Modern English Novel*, Secker & Warburg, 1993

Peter Childs, *Contemporary Novelists*, Palgrave Macmillan, 2005

Steven Connor, *The English Novel in History: 1950–1995*, Routledge, 1996

Dominic Head, *The Cambridge Introduction to Modern British Fiction, 1950–2000*, Cambridge University Press, 2002

Michael McKeon, ed., *Theory of the Novel: A Historical Approach*, Johns Hopkins University Press, 2000

Jago Morrison, *Contemporary Fiction*, Routledge, 2003

anachronistic not appropriate to the time in which it is set or shown

bathos a ludicrous descent from the elevated treatment of a subject to the ordinary and commonplace

cathartic spiritually cleansing or purifying through intense experience and feeling

character a person in a piece of writing who has consistent and developed personality traits

codicil modifying formulation added to the end of a document

coming-of-age novel novel which deals with the rites of passage or intense experiences related to the transition from childhood to adolescence or adolescence to adulthood

conceit an extended or elaborate concept that forges an unexpected connection between two apparently dissimilar things

deconstructionist critical approach which employs close analysis of a text in an attempt to unpick it and find a plurality of meanings within it. It is an application of **post-structuralism** which locates all meaning(s) within the text and does not attempt to depend on outside influences

denouement ending of a **narrative** or drama in which matters are explained or resolved

dialogue exchange of spoken words between two (or more) characters

dramatic tension sustained expectation or suspense which keeps the audience or reader anxious to know the outcome of an action or situation

ellipsis printed character consisting of three dots which indicates text has been omitted, or time passes while a character pauses in speech

empathise (with) have fellow feeling with

epilogue additional material, often explanatory or expository, at the end of a piece of writing

epistemological relating to the study of knowledge

farce comic play characterised by ridiculous action and slapstick humour

feminist criticism criticism that seeks to describe and interpret women's experience as depicted in and mediated through literary texts

first-person narrator a **narrator** who speaks in the first person, saying 'I'. A first-person narrator is not necessarily a participant in the events related

historical novel novel set in a historical period, with the cultural, social, economic and/or political setting of the period playing a significant part in the development of the action and **characters**

icon a picture or image, which stands for something else or acts as a reminder of something else

identify (with a character) emotionally align oneself with a **character** in a work of literature

idiom a word or phrase specific to the language or culture from which it comes, which has a different meaning from what is expected

imagery descriptive language which uses images to make actions, objects and **characters** more vivid in the reader's mind. Metaphors and similes are examples of imagery

irony the humorous or sarcastic use of words to imply the opposite of what they normally mean; incongruity between what might be expected and what actually happens; the ill-timed arrival of an event that had been hoped for

leitmotif recurring image or theme that accumulates meaning through repeated use

Marxist criticism criticism which seeks to adapt the socio-political and economic ideology of Karl Marx (1818–83) to a reading methodology. After the Hungarian Georg Lukács (1885-1971), Marxist criticism concentrates on the depiction of social class structures, struggles and injustice. Marxist criticism relates the content of a work to the social shifts it represents or which produced it. More recent Marxist critics have concentrated on the 'gaps' in a text, and on what is left unsaid, as its more revealing aspects

mediated presented through a medium, which may be another **character**'s consciousness or a form of writing, for example

metafiction fictional framework which contains and informs a fictional **narrative**. If one character tells a story in the context of their own narrative, the story is enclosed by the metafiction of the surrounding narrative

modernism a move away from established structures and models to embrace the experimental and avant-garde in form and content

motif a recurring idea in a work, which is used to draw the reader's attention to a particular theme or topic

mystery story in which a mystery is posed, often an unsolved crime, and the **protagonists** and reader move towards solving the mystery by noticing clues and making deductions

narrative a story, tale or any recital of events, and the manner in which it is told. First-person narratives ('I') are told from the **character's** perspective and usually require the reader to judge carefully what is being said; second-person narratives ('you') suggest the reader is part of the story; in third-person narratives ('he, 'she', 'they') the **narrator** may be intrusive (continually commenting on the story), impersonal or **omniscient**. More than one style of narrative may be used in a text

narrator the voice telling the story or relating a sequence of events

omniscient narrator a **narrator** who uses the third-person narrative and has a god-like knowledge of events and of the thoughts and feelings of the characters

pathetic arousing pathos, or pity

popular fiction fiction that lays claim to no literary merit but which is written for a mass audience, often in a popular genre such as romance, crime, horror or science fiction

postmodern move into more radical and experimental forms of writing and criticism in which the structures and functions of literature are directly questioned within a work. Postmodern writing is often self-referential, and plays with the conventions and forms of established literature

post-structuralism movement that finds fault with the premises of **structuralism** and tends to show that there are no definite and stable meanings in a text or even a word. It allows a plurality of views or meanings to coexist and denies the possibility of a single, objective truth

protagonist the principal **character** in a work of literature

reader-response critical school which gives pre-eminence to the reader's contribution in constructing meaning in a text by means of what they bring to a reading of it

resolution events which form the outcome of the action in a literary work, with all problems, dilemmas and mysteries brought to completion

rhetorical question question which is posed with the intention of drawing attention to a dilemma, conundrum, philosophical point or anomaly with no expectation that it will be answered

Romantic poet poet writing in the tradition of Samuel Taylor Coleridge and William Wordsworth in the last years of the eighteenth and early decades of the nineteenth centuries. The English Romantic poets rejected the formal structures and ostentatiously poetic language of earlier poetry written in the classical and neoclassical traditions in order to write freely and subjectively about feelings, nature and personal experience using everyday language

stream of consciousness writing which presents thoughts as they occur to a **character** or **narrator** with no overt attempts to link or structure them

structuralism movement concerned with the methods of communication and the ways that meaning is constructed into signs (such as words). It finds that literature does not reflect a pre-existing and unique reality of its own but is built up from other conventions and texts

symbol an item or figure used to represent something else. There must be some type of similarity between the symbol and what it symbolises, so that the symbol throws light on the nature of the thing symbolised or communicates its meaning in some way

tragedy originally a drama dealing with elevated actions and emotions and **characters** of high social standing in which a terrible outcome becomes inevitable as a result of a sequence of events and the personality of the main character. Classical dramatists in Greece and Rome and later European writers such as Shakespeare adhered to this model of tragedy. More recently, tragedy has come to include courses of events happening to ordinary individuals which are inevitable because of social and cultural conditions or natural disasters. Writers of this type of tragedy include the Norwegian Henrik Ibsen (1828–1906), the Russian Anton Chekhov (1860–1904) and Americans Arthur Miller (1915–2005) and Eugene O'Neill (1888–1953)

trope form of words or expression which is repeated for a particular effect

Anne Rooney taught English at the Universities of Cambridge and York before becoming a full-time writer. She has published over eighty books, including GCSE and A Level guides, and is a Royal Literary Fund Fellow at Anglia Ruskin University in Cambridge.

NOTES

GCSE

Maya Angelou
I Know Why the Caged Bird Sings

Jane Austen
Pride and Prejudice

Alan Ayckbourn
Absent Friends

Elizabeth Barrett Browning
Selected Poems

Robert Bolt
A Man for All Seasons

Harold Brighouse
Hobson's Choice

Charlotte Brontë
Jane Eyre

Emily Brontë
Wuthering Heights

Brian Clark
Whose Life is it Anyway?

Robert Cormier
Heroes

Shelagh Delaney
A Taste of Honey

Charles Dickens
David Copperfield
Great Expectations
Hard Times
Oliver Twist
Selected Stories

Roddy Doyle
Paddy Clarke Ha Ha Ha

George Eliot
Silas Marner
The Mill on the Floss

Anne Frank
The Diary of a Young Girl

William Golding
Lord of the Flies

Oliver Goldsmith
She Stoops to Conquer

Willis Hall
The Long and the Short and the Tall

Thomas Hardy
Far from the Madding Crowd
The Mayor of Casterbridge
Tess of the d'Urbervilles
The Withered Arm and other Wessex Tales

L. P. Hartley
The Go-Between

Seamus Heaney
Selected Poems

Susan Hill
I'm the King of the Castle

Barry Hines
A Kestrel for a Knave

Louise Lawrence
Children of the Dust

Harper Lee
To Kill a Mockingbird

Laurie Lee
Cider with Rosie

Arthur Miller
The Crucible
A View from the Bridge

Robert O'Brien
Z for Zachariah

Frank O'Connor
My Oedipus Complex and Other Stories

George Orwell
Animal Farm

J. B. Priestley
An Inspector Calls
When We Are Married

Willy Russell
Educating Rita
Our Day Out

J. D. Salinger
The Catcher in the Rye

William Shakespeare
Henry IV Part I
Henry V
Julius Caesar
Macbeth
The Merchant of Venice
A Midsummer Night's Dream
Much Ado About Nothing
Romeo and Juliet
The Tempest
Twelfth Night

George Bernard Shaw
Pygmalion

Mary Shelley
Frankenstein

R. C. Sherriff
Journey's End

Rukshana Smith
Salt on the Snow

John Steinbeck
Of Mice and Men

Robert Louis Stevenson
Dr Jekyll and Mr Hyde

Jonathan Swift
Gulliver's Travels

Robert Swindells
Daz 4 Zoe

Mildred D. Taylor
Roll of Thunder, Hear My Cry

Mark Twain
Huckleberry Finn

James Watson
Talking in Whispers

Edith Wharton
Ethan Frome

William Wordsworth
Selected Poems

A Choice of Poets

Mystery Stories of the Nineteenth Century including The Signalman

Nineteenth Century Short Stories

Poetry of the First World War

Six Women Poets

For the AQA Anthology:

Duffy and Armitage & Pre-1914 Poetry

Heaney and Clarke & Pre-1914 Poetry

Poems from Different Cultures

Key Stage 3

William Shakespeare

Henry V
Macbeth
Much Ado About Nothing
Richard III
The Tempest

Margaret Atwood
Cat's Eye
The Handmaid's Tale

Jane Austen
Emma
Mansfield Park
Persuasion
Pride and Prejudice
Sense and Sensibility

William Blake
Songs of Innocence and of
Experience

Charlotte Brontë
Jane Eyre
Villette

Emily Brontë
Wuthering Heights

Angela Carter
Nights at the Circus
Wise Children

Geoffrey Chaucer
The Franklin's Prologue and Tale
The Merchant's Prologue and
Tale
The Miller's Prologue and Tale
The Prologue to the Canterbury
Tales
The Wife of Bath's Prologue and
Tale

Samuel Coleridge
Selected Poems

Joseph Conrad
Heart of Darkness

Daniel Defoe
Moll Flanders

Charles Dickens
Bleak House
Great Expectations
Hard Times

Emily Dickinson
Selected Poems

John Donne
Selected Poems

Carol Ann Duffy
Selected Poems
The World's Wife

George Eliot
Middlemarch
The Mill on the Floss

T. S. Eliot
Selected Poems
The Waste Land

F. Scott Fitzgerald
The Great Gatsby

John Ford
'Tis Pity She's a Whore

E. M. Forster
A Passage to India

Michael Frayn
Spies

Charles Frazier
Cold Mountain

Brian Friel
Making History
Translations

William Golding
The Spire

Thomas Hardy
Jude the Obscure
The Mayor of Casterbridge
The Return of the Native
Selected Poems
Tess of the d'Urbervilles

Seamus Heaney
Selected Poems from 'Opened
Ground'

Nathaniel Hawthorne
The Scarlet Letter

Homer
The Iliad
The Odyssey

Aldous Huxley
Brave New World

Kazuo Ishiguro
The Remains of the Day

Ben Jonson
The Alchemist

James Joyce
Dubliners

John Keats
Selected Poems

Philip Larkin
High Windows
The Whitsun Weddings and
Selected Poems

Ian McEwan
Atonement

Christopher Marlowe
Doctor Faustus
Edward II

Arthur Miller
All My Sons
Death of a Salesman

John Milton
Paradise Lost Books I & II

Toni Morrison
Beloved

George Orwell
Nineteen Eighty-Four

Sylvia Plath
Selected Poems

William Shakespeare
Antony and Cleopatra
As You Like It
Hamlet
Henry IV Part I
King Lear
Macbeth
Measure for Measure
The Merchant of Venice
A Midsummer Night's Dream
Much Ado About Nothing
Othello
Richard II
Richard III
Romeo and Juliet
The Taming of the Shrew
The Tempest
Twelfth Night
The Winter's Tale

Mary Shelley
Frankenstein

Richard Brinsley Sheridan
The School for Scandal

Bram Stoker
Dracula

Jonathan Swift
Gulliver's Travels and A Modest
Proposal

Alfred Tennyson
Selected Poems

Alice Walker
The Color Purple

John Webster
The Duchess of Malfi

Oscar Wilde
The Importance of Being
Earnest
A Woman of No Importance

Tennessee Williams
Cat on a Hot Tin Roof
The Glass Menagerie
A Streetcar Named Desire

Jeanette Winterson
Oranges Are Not the Only Fruit

Virginia Woolf
To the Lighthouse

William Wordsworth
The Prelude and Selected Poems

W. B. Yeats
Selected Poems